OCT 28 1993

P9-BZB-473

DEMCO

PROPERTY OF
BOURBONNAIS PUBLIC LIBRARY

SITTING BULL

NORTH AMERICAN INDIANS OF ACHIEVEMENT

SITTING BULL

Chief of the Sioux

Bob Bernotas

Senior Consulting Editor
W. David Baird
Howard A. White Professor of History
Pepperdine University

CHELSEA HOUSE PUBLISHERS

New York Philadelphia

FRONTISPIECE   In 1888, inside a studio in present-day Bismarck, North Dakota, Sitting Bull donned a full headdress and posed for David F. Barry.

ON THE COVER An illustration by Vilma Ortiz of Sitting Bull holding a pipe, pipe tamper, and pipe bag, which would have been used to hold a substance for smoking, such as *kinnickinnick*, as well as to carry the disassembled pipe and tamper.

Chelsea House Publishers
EDITOR-IN-CHIEF   Remmel Nunn
MANAGING EDITOR   Karyn Gullen Browne
COPY CHIEF   Juliann Barbato
PICTURE EDITOR   Adrian G. Allen
ART DIRECTOR   Maria Epes
DEPUTY COPY CHIEF   Mark Rifkin
ASSISTANT ART DIRECTOR   Noreen Romano
MANUFACTURING MANAGER   Gerald Levine
SYSTEMS MANAGER   Lindsey Ottman
PRODUCTION MANAGER   Joseph Romano
PRODUCTION COORDINATOR   Marie Claire Cebrián

North American Indians of Achievement
SENIOR EDITOR   Liz Sonneborn

Staff for SITTING BULL
ASSISTANT EDITOR   Leigh Hope Wood
COPY EDITOR   Brian Sookram
EDITORIAL ASSISTANT   Michele Haddad
DESIGNER   Debora Smith
PICTURE RESEARCHER   Wendy Wills
COVER ILLUSTRATION   Vilma Ortiz

Copyright © 1992 by Chelsea House Publishers, a division of Main Line Book Co. All rights reserved. Printed and bound in Mexico.

3   5   7   9   8   6   4   2

Library of Congress Cataloging-in-Publication Data

Bernotas, Bob.
Sitting Bull/by Bob Bernotas
p. cm.—(North American Indians of Achievement)
Includes bibliographical references and index.
ISBN   0-7910-1703-6
        0-7910-1968-3
1. Sitting Bull, 1831–90. 2. Dakota Indians — Biography. 3. Dakota Indians — Wars.   [1. Sitting Bull, 1831–90. 2. Dakota Indians — Biography. 3. Indians of North America — Biography.] I. Title. II. Series.
E99.D1S5625 1991
978'.00497502—dc20   91-7372
[B]   CIP
[92]   AC

CONTENTS

NORTH AMERICAN INDIANS OF ACHIEVEMENT

BLACK HAWK
Sac Rebel

JOSEPH BRANT
Mohawk Chief

COCHISE
Apache Chief

CRAZY HORSE
Sioux War Chief

CHIEF GALL
Sioux War Chief

GERONIMO
Apache Warrior

HIAWATHA
Founder of the Iroquois
Confederacy

CHIEF JOSEPH
Nez Percé Leader

PETER MACDONALD
Former Chairman of the Navajo
Nation

WILMA MANKILLER
Principal Chief of the Cherokees

OSCEOLO
Seminole Rebel

QUANAH PARKER
Comanche Chief

KING PHILIP
Wampanoag Rebel

**POCAHONTAS AND CHIEF
POWHATAN**
Leaders of the Powhatan Tribes

PONTIAC
Ottawa Rebel

RED CLOUD
Sioux War Chief

WILL ROGERS
Cherokee Entertainer

SEQUOYAH
Inventor of the Cherokee Alphabet

SITTING BULL
Chief of the Sioux

TECUMSEH
Shawnee Rebel

JIM THORPE
Sac and Fox Athlete

SARAH WINNEMUCCA
Northern Paiute Writer and
Diplomat

Other titles in preparation

ON INDIAN LEADERSHIP

by W. David Baird

Howard A. White Professor of History

Pepperdine University

Authoritative utterance is in thy mouth, perception is in thy heart, and thy tongue is the shrine of justice," the ancient Egyptians said of their king. From him, the Egyptians expected authority, discretion, and just behavior. Homer's *Iliad* suggests that the Greeks demanded somewhat different qualities from their leaders: justice and judgment, wisdom and counsel, shrewdness and cunning, valor and action. It is not surprising that different people living at different times should seek different qualities from the individuals they looked to for guidance. By and large, a people's requirements for leadership are determined by two factors: their culture and the unique circumstances of the time and place in which they live.

Before the late 15th century, when non-Indians first journeyed to what is now North America, most Indian tribes were not ruled by a single person. Instead, there were village chiefs, clan headmen, peace chiefs, war chiefs, and a host of other types of leaders, each with his or her own specific duties. These influential people not only decided political matters but also helped shape their tribe's social, cultural, and religious life. Usually, Indian leaders held their positions because they had won the respect of their peers. Indeed, if a leader's followers at any time decided that he or she was out of step with the will of the people, they felt free to look to someone else for advice and direction.

Thus, the greatest achievers in traditional Indian communities were men and women of extraordinary talent. They were not only skilled at navigating the deadly waters of tribal politics and cultural customs but also able to, directly or indirectly, make a positive and significant difference in the daily life of their followers.

7

From the beginning of their interaction with Native Americans, non-Indians failed to understand these features of Indian leadership. Early European explorers and settlers merely assumed that Indians had the same relationship with their leaders as non-Indians had with their kings and queens. European monarchs generally inherited their positions and ruled large nations however they chose, often with little regard for the desires or needs of their subjects. As a result, the settlers of Jamestown saw Pocahontas as a "princess" and Pilgrims dubbed Wampanoag leader Metacom "King Philip," envisioning them in roles very different from those in which their own people placed them.

As more and more non-Indians flocked to North America, the nature of Indian leadership gradually began to change. Influential Indians no longer had to take on the often considerable burden of pleasing only their own people; they also had to develop a strategy of dealing with the non-Indian newcomers. In a rapidly changing world, new types of Indian role models with new ideas and talents continually emerged. Some were warriors; others were peacemakers. Some held political positions within their tribes; others were writers, artists, religious prophets, or athletes. Although the demands of Indian leadership altered from generation to generation, several factors that determined which Indian people became prominent in the centuries after first contact remained the same.

Certain personal characteristics distinguished these Indians of achievement. They were intelligent, imaginative, practical, daring, shrewd, uncompromising, and logical. They were constant in friendships, unrelenting in hatreds, affectionate with their relatives, and respectful to their God or gods. Of course, no single Native American leader embodied all these qualities, nor these qualities only. But it was these characteristics that allowed them to succeed.

The special skills and talents that certain Indians possessed also brought them to positions of importance. The life of Hiawatha, the legendary founder of the powerful Iroquois Confederacy, displays the value that oratorical ability had for many Indians in power. The biography of Cochise, the 19th-century Apache chief, illustrates that leadership often required keen diplomatic skills not only in transactions among tribespeople but also in hardheaded negotiations with non-Indians. For others, such as Mohawk Joseph Brant and Navajo Peter MacDonald, a non-Indian education proved advantageous in their dealings with other peoples.

Sudden changes in circumstance were another crucial factor in determining who became influential in Indian communities. King Philip in the 1670s and Geronimo in the 1880s both came to power when their people were searching for someone to lead them into battle against white frontiersmen who had forced upon them a long series of indignities. Seeing the rising discontent of Indians of many tribes in the 1810s, Tecumseh and his brother, the Shawnee prophet Tenskwatawa, proclaimed a message of cultural revitalization that appealed to thousands. Other Indian achievers recognized cooperation with non-Indians as the most advantageous path during their lifetime. Sarah Winnemucca in the late 19th century bridged the gap of understanding between her people and their non-Indian neighbors through the publication of her autobiography *Life Among the Piutes*. Olympian Jim Thorpe in the early 20th century championed the assimilationist policies of the U.S. government and, with his own successes, demonstrated the accomplishments Indians could make in the non-Indian world. And Wilma Mankiller, principal chief of the Cherokees, continues to fight successfully for the rights of her people through the courts and through negotiation with federal officials.

Leadership among Native Americans, just as among all other peoples, can be understood only in the context of culture and history. But the centuries that Indians have had to cope with invasions of foreigners in their homelands have brought unique hardships and obstacles to the Native American individuals who most influenced and inspired others. Despite these challenges, there has never been a lack of Indian men and women equal to these tasks. With such strong leaders, it is no wonder that Native Americans remain such a vital part of this nation's cultural landscape.

1

A NEW CHIEF

In 1867, the people of the Hunkpapa Sioux were greatly troubled. Life on the northern Plains had grown difficult, almost impossible. Harsh weather, wars with other Indian nations, and treaties that the United States government made and then broke had brought on hard times for these proud and self-sufficient buffalo hunters. They were having trouble feeding themselves. So, they began to question the authority of their four chiefs.

The people of any society, when confronted with such hardship, inevitably look to their leadership. The Hunkpapa people did not like what they saw. They felt that the character of the four chiefs was not what it should be. A chief was supposed to be dignified, tolerant, generous, and above spite or pettiness. He should be quick to forgive and slow to lose his temper. It was not unusual for the Sioux tribes to select a chief for his kind and gentle qualities, even though he may not have been a warrior of much renown. A man who was a great warrior might even turn down a chieftaincy because he felt that he lacked the necessary qualities of humanity and compassion.

Sitting Bull, photographed by David F. Barry. Recognized as both a skillful peacemaker and a brave Hunkpapa warrior, Sitting Bull, at the age of 36, was inaugurated chief of all the Teton Sioux tribes.

Because of their behavior, the four chiefs had lost the respect of their people. Running Antelope and Red Horn had stolen other men's wives. Loud-Voiced Hawk had

11

stabbed and killed another Sioux. Only one of the chiefs, Four Horns, was not directly involved in any scandal. Still, the conduct of his three colleagues shamed Four Horns, and the people were criticizing him because of his association with the other chiefs.

So, the headmen of the tribe devised a test of their leaders' fitness. They wanted to see how the chiefs would respond if someone tried to steal their wives. Running Antelope, Red Horn, and Loud-Voiced Hawk all reacted violently, displaying the weakness and passions of ordinary men. The Plains Indians, however, could not afford to have ordinary men as their chiefs.

Only Four Horns maintained his dignity, proving that of the four, he alone deserved to be chief. Still, he was disturbed and humiliated by the disgrace that the others had brought on the high office that they shared. Four Horns decided that he must select a new chief, a single leader who would restore the honor of, and rebuild the people's respect in, the chieftaincy. In his view, only one man among all the Hunkpapa Sioux warriors possessed the necessary qualities of leadership — his nephew, Sitting Bull.

Then in his mid-thirties, Sitting Bull was well known among his people as an able buffalo hunter and a brave warrior who usually led the charges against the enemy. More important, he was a popular figure in the camp, a kind man whose talent for settling disputes among his people had earned him a reputation as a peacemaker. He displayed a fair mind and a determination to do things his own way. He tempered his bravery with mercy; on numerous occasions he spared the life of unlucky victims and even enemies of the Sioux. Courage and cruelty, Sitting Bull realized, seldom go together.

Sitting Bull was also famous for his generosity toward the poor and weak of the tribe; he shared his food, and even gave away many of his horses. Although as a warrior he had received many honors, he never behaved with arrogance or conceit but truly was a "man of the people." A sociable young man, Sitting Bull always was ready with a story or a joke, and the people particularly admired his ability to make up and sing songs. Devoutly religious, he usually got what he prayed for, and his gift of prophecy was uncanny.

Four Horns felt that, given this unique combination of attributes, his nephew would be able to guide the Hunkpapas through the troubled times that lay ahead. The other tribal leaders agreed. They believed that the qualities of a man who was killed entered the body of his slayer. Sitting Bull had once killed a Crow chief in battle; it was no surprise, they reasoned, that this warrior had the character of a chief. Four Horns's nomination of Sitting Bull was accepted unanimously by the headmen of the Hunkpapa Sioux.

Drawing by Sitting Bull depicting his battle with a Crow chief. The Sioux believed that Sitting Bull, having killed a chief, had taken on the qualities necessary to command a nation.

The Hunkpapas were just one of seven Sioux tribes
that roamed and hunted throughout the northern Plains,
the region now occupied by the states of South and North
Dakota. These tribes — the Blackfoot Sioux (who were
not related to the northern Blackfoot Indians), Brules,
Hunkpapas, Minneconjous, Oglalas, Sans-Arcs, and Two-
Kettles — spoke similar languages and considered themselves relatives and allies, but they were autonomous
bodies. They were known collectively as the Teton, or
Lakota, Sioux.

Up until this time, individual Teton chiefs waged war
or made peace at their own discretion. As a result,
relations among the Teton Sioux and the other Indians
of the Plains, as well as between the Teton tribes and
non-Indians, had become dangerously uncertain. When
approaching an Indian camp or army fort, one never
knew whether to expect a friendly or a hostile reception.

Four Horns and the Hunkpapa warrior societies felt
the interests of all the Teton Sioux could be served best
by a single head chief. This man would be responsible
for organizing hunting parties and defending the northern Plains against both enemy tribes and the increasing
encroachment of the whites. They proposed that this head
chief should be Sitting Bull.

Most of the other Teton Sioux responded positively to
the Hunkpapas' proposal, as did their traditional allies,
the Cheyennes and Arapahos. As the day of Sitting Bull's
inauguration as chief approached, the Minneconjous and
Sans-Arc Sioux, as well as the Cheyennes, arrived at the
Hunkpapa camp and set up great camps of their own.
The Two-Kettles and Blackfoot Sioux were also represented, as were the Yanktonai Sioux from the south, and
the Arapahos, who camped with the Cheyennes.

The Brule Sioux, however, rejected Sitting Bull's
selection as head chief of all the Teton Sioux and did not

An engraving after a painting of a Dakota encampment by Seth Eastman. The Hunkpapa Sioux were just one of many Indian tribes that hunted in present-day North and South Dakota.

attend the ceremony. Their leader, Spotted Tail, wanted the position himself and trusted non-Indian authorities to help him attain it. At the same time, the Southern Oglalas, under their chief, Red Cloud, were preparing to sign a peace treaty with the United States. However, another band of Oglalas, headed by the famous warrior Crazy Horse, was not interested in any treaty, and joined in Sitting Bull's inauguration. Thus, the installment of Sitting Bull as head chief united the various Sioux tribes to the fullest possible extent.

The inauguration ceremony was a splendid spectacle. The four outgoing chiefs took a buffalo robe to Sitting Bull's lodge, seated him upon it, and then carried him to the special council lodge. Some two dozen chiefs, representing the numerous participating tribes, had already assembled. Once the head chief took his place of honor, the ceremony began.

A long pipe was lit. First, its mouthpiece was offered to the earth, so that the earth might hold the Sioux good and strong. Then it was offered to each of the four winds, so that no distress or ill luck should be blown upon the Sioux. Next it was offered to the sun, so that all might see their way clearly and avoid danger and death. Finally, it was passed from hand to hand, each chief taking a puff or two, blowing the smoke skyward with a prayer to his god, Wakan' Tanka. The pipe was then presented to Sitting Bull as a badge of his office. In the future, he would use it when he prayed.

Many speeches and songs followed, each one paying tribute to some aspect of Sitting Bull's character — his bravery, generosity, mercy, and kindness. Four Horns, Sitting Bull's uncle and the outgoing chief who first proposed Sitting Bull's nomination, acted as master of ceremonies. "Because of your bravery on the battlefield," he declared, "and your reputation as the bravest warrior in all our bands, we have elected you head chief of the entire Sioux nation, head war chief. It is your duty to see that the nation is fed, that we have plenty. When you say 'fight,' we shall fight; when you say 'make peace,' we shall make peace."

Now, Sitting Bull was the commander in chief of the Sioux, the principle strategist and military leader for more than 10,000 Teton Indians. Like him, these people no longer believed the white man's promises, which had all too often been broken, and objected to living restricted to a reservation.

Crazy Horse, the brave and serious-minded leader of the Oglala Sioux, was named second in command. In crises, he would assist Sitting Bull in making decisions that would affect all the Teton people. These two men were close friends and trusted each other with their lives.

Sitting Bull was presented with a bow and 10 arrows and a flintlock gun. He was told that he should study to be like the eagle, the chief of all birds, the one that flies

Spotted Tail, chief of the Brule Sioux, rejected Sitting Bull's selection as head chief of all the Teton Sioux. The Brule leader had hoped to attain the position himself by truckling to the whites.

highest. Among many Indian cultures, including that of the Sioux, eagle feathers are worn as a mark of bravery. Indeed, the ceremony reached its climax when a magnificent warbonnet of beads, ermine fur, and eagle feathers was brought out and placed on the new chief's head. Every feather represented a brave deed by the warrior who had contributed it to the bonnet. As such, the bonnet stood for the collective valor of all the Teton Sioux, symbolizing both the people's greatness and the hopes vested in their new leader.

At last, Sitting Bull was led out of the lodge and given one final gift, a beautiful white horse, the horse of a chief. After being lifted onto his horse, he rode as a chief, followed by two mighty columns of warriors, who belonged to the many warrior societies that had come to take part in the inauguration. Each rider, with his face painted as if for war, carried a decorated shield and lance. As they rode through the camp circle, the great city of the Sioux nation, the warriors chanted. The new chief then broke into a song that he had composed for the occasion:

> Ye tribes, behold me.
> The chiefs of old are gone.
> Myself, I shall take courage.

In the decades ahead, Sitting Bull would have to draw upon all his courage, as well as all his wisdom. He already could see that his people's traditional way of life was in danger. The Plains Indians were facing a new and powerful enemy, one more relentless and cruel than any they had encountered throughout their long history — white "civilization."

*A photo of the countryside sur-
rounding the Grand River,
near present-day Bullhead,
South Dakota. Sitting Bull
was born in the area in 1831
at a place known to the
Hunkpapa as Many-Caches.*

2

EARNING HIS NAME

The man called Sitting Bull was born in March 1831, near the site of present-day Bullhead, South Dakota, along the Grand River. His place of birth was known to the Hunkpapa Sioux as Many-Caches because they stored supplies there. Sitting Bull was deliberate and slightly awkward as a child. Although he would grow up to be one of the most famous Indian warriors and leaders, the child's parents could see nothing especially remarkable in him. They called him Slow. According to the Sioux custom, this would be his name until he could earn a better one for himself.

Slow's father, Returns-Again, was a great warrior; his name meant that he always returned to fight another day. Like most of the adult Sioux men, he was frequently away hunting, and so as an infant, Slow spent most of his time with his mother, Mixed Day (later known as Her-Holy-Door), and other female relatives. In the typical Sioux manner, the baby was carried by his mother strapped to a cradleboard; this allowed the mother's hands to be free, which made it easier for her to perform daily chores.

For the typical Sioux boy or girl, childhood was a happy, seemingly carefree time. Sioux parents placed few restrictions on their children's conduct. Sioux children learned the importance of discipline straight from the daily drama of survival on the northern Plains. In addition, from a very early age, Sioux children were taught to respect the ways of their ancestors. This combination of a challenging, often harsh environment and a deeply held admiration for their heritage, made strict parental control over a child's behavior unnecessary for the Sioux.

Most of the games that Slow and his boyhood friends played actually imitated the activities of their elders, such as hunting, going on raids, and making or breaking camp. As buffalo hunters who followed the huge migrating herds, the Sioux were constantly on the move and could break camp in as little as 15 minutes. Such speed was often necessary, for competition for food and horses among the Indian nations was fierce, and enemy attacks were frequent. These games therefore provided valuable training for adulthood.

War was a fact of life for the Plains Indians. It was the means through which a Sioux man earned honors and prestige within the tribe; it was also the way that a Sioux boy proved himself to be a man. Like all Sioux children, Slow was born and grew up in the midst of ambush, battle, and the constant risk of death. At the age of 10, he had already killed his first buffalo calf. Now a young, strong youth of 14, Slow yearned for real battle.

His opportunity came one day as he watched a party of warriors mount their horses and leave camp. Slow jumped onto his pony and followed them. When the precocious 14-year-old arrived at the rendezvous point, the adult warriors stared at him in silence. Slow rode up beside his father and simply told him that he was going with them. His father was surprised, but proud to see his son at his side. "You have a good running horse," he told the boy. "Try to do something brave."

Sitting Bull's mother, Mixed Day, was later known as Her-Holy-Door, possibly a reference to her having given birth to the great chief.

His father gave him a *coupstick*, a long wand used for striking the enemy. For the Sioux warrior, personal contact with a foe was all-important, even more so than the man's death. What mattered was not who killed an opponent, but who first touched the body — alive or dead — with his coupstick. This was known as "counting coup on him," a phrase borrowed from the French frontiersmen who trapped and traded with the Plains Indians.

Being the first to count coup on an enemy was the highest honor a warrior could attain. (Three other warriors could count coup on the same enemy, but this was a considerably lesser honor.) Sioux warriors competed to count the first coup on an enemy. When a man struck his foe, he would declare, "I have overcome this one"; this way, he would have witnesses to his deed. After he accomplished this, other comrades might kill and scalp the unlucky adversary. Once the battle was over, the warriors put in claims for their honors, and those who could produce witnesses were awarded the rights and privileges that went along with counting the first coup.

A warrior was entitled to wear an eagle tail feather upright in his hair for each occasion that he had counted coup on an enemy. Because the greatest warriors were quite well known within the tribe, they usually wore only one or two feathers out of modesty. However, for special ceremonies and celebrations they would don glorious warbonnets, with trains of feathers that trailed to their heels.

Counting coup also earned the winner the right to tell the stories of his heroism at the many gatherings during which Sioux warriors recounted their feats. Until a man attained this right, he was barred from participating in tribal ceremonies. He could not even name his own children. Counting coup, therefore, was expected of grown men; it was a necessary requirement of Sioux manhood. For a boy of 14 to accomplish such a feat would be

A cradleboard, when strapped on a mother's back, enables the Sioux to look after their young children while performing daily chores.

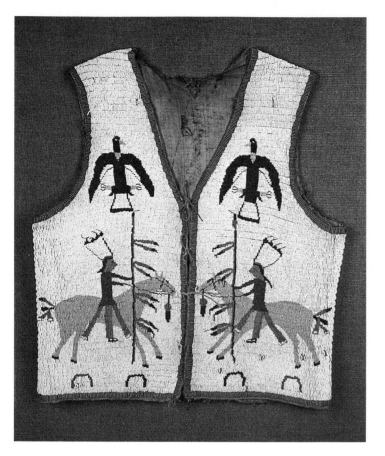

A man's beaded vest on which a warrior is shown carrying a coupstick. For the Sioux, personal contact in battle brought higher honors than did the actual killing of the opponent. A coupstick was used to strike the enemy.

astounding. Slow, however, was eager for a chance to prove himself.

The Sioux war party could see the enemy band coming, still far off. They prepared to surprise their opponents, ambushing them once they came close enough. As they lay in wait, Slow charged toward the foe on his pony. The others quickly changed their strategy and followed his lead. The enemy warriors were startled at the boldness of the attack and began to retreat.

Traveling with great speed, Slow closed in on an enemy rider, who threw himself off his mount, turned, and prepared to fire an arrow right at the reckless youth. At that instant, Slow lunged at his adversary, striking him with his father's coupstick and declaring loudly his feat. The enemy's arrow had missed its target. Immediately, other Sioux warriors set upon Slow's opponent, killing him.

After the battle the victorious Sioux band gathered up the trophies they had captured — horses, weapons, scalps — and returned to camp. When they arrived, they paraded around the camp, each warrior announcing the brave deeds that would now be added to his battle record.

Slow's father was jubilant, perhaps even more than the boy himself. His son had counted coup at an unusually early age. He called the people to behold his child, the hero of the day, the first of them all to strike at an enemy. This was a remarkable boy, he thought. Today he no longer was a child, but had become a man, one destined for great things and certainly deserving of a better name than Slow.

By this time, Slow's father had already given up the name Returns-Again because of a strange and marvelous occurrence. The Sioux were a mystical people who attached great significance to visions and dreams. Among the Hunkpapas, Returns-Again was known for his occult powers, specifically his ability to understand the language of animals.

Once, in the quiet of the prairie evening, a great bull buffalo walked toward the campfire where Returns-Again and three other hunters were eating and resting. This, they believed, was no ordinary buffalo, but the physical embodiment of the Buffalo God, one of the most important gods to the Sioux people. While his three awestruck comrades sat frozen, Returns-Again listened as the beast "spoke" to him. He grunted, "Tatan'ka Iyota'ke, Tatan'ka Psi'ca, Tatan'ka Winyu'ha Najin', Tatan'ka Wanji'la." In the Sioux language this means "Sitting Bull, Jumping Bull, Bull-Standing-with-Cow, Lone Bull." This strange

string of words, Returns-Again realized, stood for the ancient Sioux formula for the four stages of life: Infancy, Youth, Maturity, and Old Age.

The hunters reasoned that because only Returns-Again had understood the words of the Buffalo God, these four names were his to use as he wished. Although he already had a warrior's name, he discarded it and began to call himself by the first of the names that the Buffalo God had spoken, Sitting Bull. That remained his name until just after his son's first battle.

As Slow rode around camp that day, a hero in his first encounter with the enemy, his father was filled with pride. He could perform no greater act of love toward his son than to bestow upon him his own name, that which

Sitting Bull—positioned under the bull sitting on its haunches—charges his enemy on horseback and strikes him with a coupstick, earning his first honor in battle.

the Buffalo God had given to him. "My son has struck the enemy!" he declared. "He is brave! I dub him *Tatan'ka Iyota'ke*, Sitting Bull!" From that day until his death, young Sitting Bull's father was known as Jumping Bull, the second of the sacred names that he had received on that mystical night by the campfire.

An interviewer once asked a number of men who knew Sitting Bull to tell him what men the great chief most admired or was influenced by in his youth. None of the old men had anything to say, except for one, who replied indignantly, "Sitting Bull did not imitate any *man*; he imitated the buffalo." Of course, like all hunters, he had to study the habits and behavior of his prey, the buffalo. But beyond that, many people who knew Sitting Bull believed that his personality actually took on the characteristics of the animal for whom he was named.

The Indians admired the buffalo as a headstrong, stubborn creature, afraid of nothing, deterred by no obstacle, never turning back. It possessed great endurance, courage, and strength. These were the qualities — fighting qualities — that the adult Sitting Bull displayed as a hunter, a warrior, and a leader of his people. Thus, his name, the loving gift of a proud father, turned out to be extraordinarily prophetic.

3

"HE FED THE WHOLE NATION"

Despite his love of combat and the ferocity with which he fought, the young warrior Sitting Bull always tempered his courage with mercy. On one occasion, when he was about 17 years old, a war party returned from raiding the Crows. Along with the usual trophies, they brought a Crow woman.

It was the Sioux custom to absorb female captives into the camp; in time, she might become an adopted member of the tribe. However, as the men performed their victory dance, the women, in talking to the captive, learned that she was a *wit'ko-win*, a "crazy woman," one who was sexually promiscuous. Having discovered her unsavory past, the Sioux women refused to accept the captive as one of their own. As a punishment for her sins, they decided to burn her alive. They seized her, tore off her clothing, and tied her to a tree, piling dry brush around her feet.

When he learned of the women's intentions, Sitting Bull was moved with pity for the pathetic Crow prisoner. As a youth of 17, however, he was too young and too lacking in authority to stop them. There was only one thing he could do to spare the helpless woman from the horrible torture that she was facing. As the Hunkpapa

Although Sitting Bull had won many honors in battle and was afterward awarded eagle tail feathers, in this photograph by David F. Barry he modestly wears only two feathers.

27

women began to apply the flames to the dry brush, Sitting Bull took out an arrow, raised his bow, and shot the captive through the heart, killing her instantly. Although he could not save her, at least he was able to defy the mob and give the Crow woman a painless death.

As the years passed, Sitting Bull time and time again demonstrated his prowess in hunting and his bravery in combat. It was only natural that he be inducted into the Hunkpapa warrior society known as the Strong Hearts.

This headdress, which belonged to Sitting Bull's friend Crazy Horse, typifies those worn by members of the Sioux warrior society. To be a member of such a society brought great prestige.

This prestigious lodge was responsible for policing the encampments, governing hunting expeditions, and defending territorial boundaries — functions that were vital to the life of the tribe. To be a member was a great honor and a badge of a man's social status.

Sitting Bull rose quickly through the ranks of the Strong Hearts and attained the distinguished position as one of the lodge's two sash-wearers. In battle, the sash-wearers wore a bonnet covered with crow feathers, with a black buffalo horn over each of their ears and ermine streamers trailing down their back. The most significant element of the sash-wearer's regalia, however, was the strip of scarlet woolen cloth decorated with feathers. It was hung over one shoulder, extending to the ground. During an encounter with an enemy, the sash-wearers would stick a lance through the end of the sash and into the ground, actually staking themselves in one place. This act symbolized their vow to never retreat once they had taken their stand, but to hold their ground and fight until they met either victory or death. They could be released only by a comrade.

In the autumn of 1856 the Hunkpapas needed horses. Horses were essential for hunting buffalo and other large game. The Teton Sioux seldom raised their own horses, for the winters of the northern Plains were severe and foals could not survive. That left just two ways to obtain the required animals — trade for them or steal them from enemies such as the Crows. Stealing them, of course, was cheaper; more importantly, it meant battle, the chance for glory and honor. So a war party of 100 warriors, including Sitting Bull, set out along the Yellowstone River in search of enemy camps that they might raid.

They soon encountered a Crow camp and went into action. A party of men was selected to enter the camp on foot and make off with as many animals as possible.

Although these men were able to get a large number of horses and return to the encampment without a fight, all the warriors knew that they would be pursued. Hampered by the large and cumbersome herd of stolen horses, they would not be able to get very far before the Crows caught up with them. As the Sioux warriors prepared to fight, sunrise approached, bringing with it the Crow war party.

When the Crow saw the Sioux warriors lined up and ready for the attack, they held back. Only the three Crow leaders charged. The first counted coup on two Sioux and then got away. The second killed a Sioux warrior. The third was confronted by Sitting Bull.

Jumping off his horse he yelled, "Come on! I'll fight you. I am Sitting Bull." As the Crow ran toward him, Sitting Bull could see that he was wearing a red shirt trimmed with ermine, the insignia of a chief, and that he carried a flintlock gun. When the Crow chief saw Sitting Bull's sash-wearer regalia, he knew that he, too, would face a man of great bravery. Running forward to meet the enemy, Sitting Bull sang a Strong Hearts song:

> Comrades, whoever runs away,
> He is a woman, they say;
> Therefore, through many trials,
> My life is short!

In his new muzzle-loader there was only one shot; he would have to make it count.

The Crow chief fired first. Sitting Bull threw up his shield, an effective deterrent against arrows, but little protection against gunfire. First the ball pierced his shield, and then the sole of his left foot. Although painfully wounded, Sitting Bull fired, and the enemy fell. He removed his long knife from its scabbard and plunged it into the heart of the dying Crow.

The death of their leader terrified the Crows. They retreated, and immediately the Hunkpapas charged, routing the Crows and counting many coups. Afterward, Sitting Bull's wound was treated, but it did not heal well, and for the rest of his life he walked with a limp. His impaired walk, though, was a badge of honor, a trophy won before 100 witnesses, a constant and unforgettable reminder of his battle with a Crow chief.

Soon after, the Strong Hearts chose to honor this hero. Within the society there was an elite group, the Midnight Strong Hearts, the cream of the warrior lodge. They named Sitting Bull their leader, which effectively made him chief of the Strong Hearts, a high honor for a man just 25 years old.

Within the Hunkpapa Sioux, Sitting Bull, as chief of the Strong Hearts, was in charge of all matters related to hunting. Many years after his death, the old men who

Indians Hunting the Bison, *painted by Karl Bodmer in the 1830s. Sitting Bull, like other Plains Indians, respected the buffalo for its fighting qualities and depended on it for his livelihood.*

knew Sitting Bull in his prime would recall with admiration, "He fed the whole nation." However, Sitting Bull never killed animals indiscriminately. Being a Plains Indian, he regarded the animals he hunted as fellow creatures. The Indians hunted out of necessity, so they could eat. To slaughter animals wastefully would be the lowest form of ingratitude, they believed, for these creatures gave up their life so that the people could survive. Unfortunately, as the Indians came to realize, this kind of deep respect for nature and wildlife was foreign to the white man's culture.

The buffalo was the cornerstone of the Plains Indians' existence. Besides relying on the animal for food, the Indians needed its heavy skin to cover their homes (known as "tipis"). They also used the hides, as well as the buffalo's fur and sinew, to make robes and other types of clothing. It was Sitting Bull's responsibility to both organize and supervise several hunting expeditions each year, so that the tribe would have sufficient supplies of these necessities.

Competition for buffalo was fierce among the tribes of the Plains. Often the herds became scarce. In order to enlarge the hunting range of the Sioux, Sitting Bull had to lead his people into battle against the Crow, Arikara, Mandan, Gros Ventre, Hidatsa, Assiniboin (also known as the Hohes), Blackfoot, Flathead, Piegran, and Shoshone Indians. By defeating these other Plains tribes, Sitting Bull could secure for his people a plentiful supply of food and the other buffalo-borne essentials.

As the winter of 1857 neared, Sitting Bull and a Hunkpapa Sioux war party went out in pursuit of their bitter, long time enemies, the Assiniboins, or Hohes. However, all they found was a single Assiniboin tipi — just 1 family, a father and mother and their 3 sons, the youngest a baby, the oldest no more than 11 years of age.

The Sioux warriors had no qualms about killing enemy women and children. After all, each of them had lost family members to enemy arrows. Furthermore, to kill a woman in the presence of her husband was considered a brave deed.

The unfortunate Assiniboin family saw the approaching Sioux and tried to flee, but they were doomed. In no time, the father, mother, and the two youngest children were dead. Only the tall 11-year-old was still alive. Having seen his family slaughtered, he turned and faced the warriors, took out his little bow and arrow, and began to fire, hopelessly, until all his arrows were gone. Surrounded by his enemies, facing imminent death, the boy did not cry. His eyes picked out the face of Sitting Bull from among the hostile crowd, and he called to him, "Big Brother."

Sitting Bull had observed the boy's courage and was moved. Perhaps the Strong Hearts' chief saw something of himself at that age. Maybe he was thinking of the gap left in his life by the recent death of his wife and small son. Filled with both pity and admiration, Sitting Bull flung his arms around the boy, shielding the child from the arrows of his own warriors.

"Don't shoot!" he cried. "This boy is too brave to die. I have no brother. I will take this one for my brother. Let him live."

Some of the other Sioux were reluctant to spare the boy. He was the enemy, they felt, and he did try to shoot at them, however feebly. Sitting Bull would not budge, though; he was going to adopt the boy and that was final. The boy, so well treated, had no wish to return to the Assiniboin camp and his relatives. For this reason, Sitting Bull named him Stays-Back.

It was not uncommon for a prominent adult warrior to adopt a younger, less-favored male as his brother.

S.B.   "Hohé"

Among the Sioux, generosity was one of the most highly prized qualities. To possess wealth alone meant very little. One earned distinction within the tribe not for being wealthy, but for giving one's possessions away to those who were less fortunate. In other words, the practice of dispersing wealth was more highly esteemed than the practice of accumulating wealth. By adopting the orphaned Assiniboin boy, Sitting Bull not only demonstrated his well-known kindness and generosity, but brought great honor on himself as well.

The Sioux adoption ceremony reflected this emphasis on giving. As part of the ritual, a medicine man bound Sitting Bull and the young boy with leather thongs to

In this drawing by No Two Horns, Sitting Bull wears the headdress of the Strong Hearts warrior society. The chief is shown sparing the life of an Assiniboin boy, whom he embraced as a brother and protected from the other Sioux warriors.

symbolize the duties and obligations that this relationship entailed. Thereafter their fortunes would be bound together. The wish of one would be the law of the other. From then on, each must give preference to his brother before anyone else and be willing to do anything for, or give anything to, the other.

The ceremony was followed by a lavish feast, at which the host, Sitting Bull, provided great quantities of food and gave presents — including the most valuable of all, horses — to those less wealthy. When the day was over, Sitting Bull was a much poorer man, but he had taken another step upward in the Sioux hierarchy. At the age of 26, he was chief of the Strong Hearts, from which he derived great power, and he had sponsored a *hunka*, an adopted member of the band, for which he gained much prestige. Over time, the story of Sitting Bull having saved the life of the helpless boy became as famous as the tales of his exploits in battle. Long after his death, the old men who knew Sitting Bull often mused that in sparing that helpless enemy, he had showed the heart of a great chief.

The following June, Sitting Bull's father, Jumping Bull, was killed in a Crow ambush. Jumping Bull was no longer a young man; ill and suffering from a chronic and painful toothache, he despised his enfeebled condition. He had lived as a warrior and now wanted to die as one. When the Crows attacked, he was one of the first Hunkpapas to engage a Crow warrior in single combat. Of course he was in no condition to be fighting hand-to-hand against a much younger man, and he was killed. Still, it was the kind of death he had wanted, death on the field of battle.

When Sitting Bull heard that his father was dead, he raced after the Crow who was responsible, overtook him, and killed him. The Hunkpapas were angry and ashamed that the Crows were able to ambush them so easily, so they charged off after the attackers, chasing them for 30 miles. When they caught up, a fierce battle ensued, in which 2 Sioux and 10 Crows were killed. Sitting Bull, fueled by his sorrow over the death of Jumping Bull, fought recklessly. Finally, the Crows fled, leaving behind three women and a child, whom the Sioux took as captives.

The warriors who had taken the captives were very bitter about Jumping Bull's death. The old man had been a great warrior, respected by all; his son, Sitting Bull, was their friend, and they were moved to sympathy by his distress. As revenge for the death of Jumping Bull, they decided to kill the captive Crow women.

Sitting Bull suspected their plans and insisted that they not seek vengeance for his sake. He knew that the women had lost husbands and brothers in the battle, and they were as stricken with grief as he. "Treat them well and let them live," he told his friends. "My father was a man, and death is his." At the end of the summer, the Crow women were returned to their camp, along with a number of good horses, according to the wishes of Sitting Bull.

After Jumping Bull's death, Sitting Bull gave the fallen warrior's name to his adopted brother, who in time bestowed great distinction upon the name in his own right. In battle, the young Jumping Bull proved himself to be brave and fierce. He eventually became chief of the Strong Hearts, the position held by his brother and mentor. To the end, he remained loyal to Sitting Bull.

When the Civil War broke out in 1861, the white fur traders, most of whom were Southern sympathizers, tried to get the Teton Sioux to fight against the Union troops. Although they had many grievances against the federal government, the Sioux asked no more than to be left alone. Sitting Bull consistently avoided contact with all whites, except for the traders. As long as they did not violate the sanctuary of his people, Sitting Bull refused to lead his Hunkpapa Strong Hearts against them. He had not reacted when military posts were set up all along the Missouri River in 1856 or when the founding of the Dakota Territory in 1861 encroached on the eastern edge of the Black Hills. However, by 1863, Sitting Bull would be forced to abandon this policy of peaceful coexistence with the whites.

To the east, in what is now the state of Minnesota, the Santee Sioux, under the leadership of Little Crow, had been engaged in a fierce war with U.S. troops and white settlers. A battle between the Santees and the settlers in the town of New Ulm ended with 100 whites dead. This was followed by indiscriminate slaughtering of settlers by marauding bands of Santee, who were not under the control of Little Crow. Although Sitting Bull's Hunkpapas were located well to the west of these hostilities, the so-called Minnesota Massacre eventually embroiled the whole Sioux nation in war with the whites.

In June 1863, General Henry Hastings Sibley, leading a punitive expedition into Hunkpapa country in pursuit of Santee refugees, attacked Sitting Bull's hunting party east of the Missouri River. Sitting Bull retaliated by skirmishing with Sibley's wagon train. It was the first time Sitting Bull had fought against whites, but he did not consider himself at war with them as yet. He moved his band westward and resumed hunting.

The following summer, Sitting Bull's people were camped near the Killdeer Mountains. Other Sioux bands joined the camp until, in time, there were hundreds of lodges representing nearly every Teton tribe. Some of the new arrivals brought disturbing news that quickly spread through the camp — soldiers, perhaps thousands of them, were coming up the Missouri. The Tetons were deeply concerned.

Then, a party of Yanktonai and Santee Sioux from the east came and pitched their lodges near Sitting Bull's camp. Sitting Bull's nephew, Bull-Standing-with-Cow (who was later known as Chief Joseph White Bull), heard that the soldiers were chasing Yanktonais and Santees. A few days later the troops arrived, a mile-long line of them on foot and on horseback. Their commander was General Alfred Sully.

With rifles and cannons, the troops attacked the massed tribes. The Sioux, armed only with bows, lances, clubs, and muskets, stood their ground and successfully repelled the assault. Sitting Bull was filled with pride for his nation. The Battle of Killdeer Mountain, July 28, 1864, marked a turning point in his life. Whether or not he wanted to be, he was now at war with the army of the United States.

To the Indians, the white man's method of war was a dull affair. For the Sioux, the aim of battle was personal contact with the enemy, to strike him with the hand. Killing a foe from a long range with bullets brought no glory, it counted no coups. This kind of warfare was "just shooting."

Further, the white man's war spent precious ammunition that the Indians might use to better purpose in hunting buffalo and other large game. As hostilities between the Indians and the government intensified, it became increasingly difficult for Indians to obtain bullets. The authorities feared, in many instances quite rightly, that the bullets would be used against U.S. troops. But for the most part, whatever ammunition the Indians did obtain was used for hunting — not warfare.

Sitting Bull's first encounters with the U.S. soldiers left him unimpressed with their fighting ability. "The white soldiers do not know how to fight," he criticized. "They are not lively enough. They stand still and run straight;

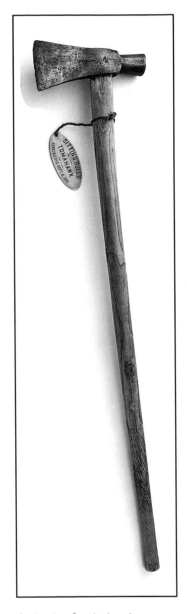

In battles fought hand-to-hand, the Sioux used weapons such as this tomahawk, once owned by Sitting Bull. They preferred to save their precious bullets for hunting.

it is easy to shoot them." He also felt that they treated their own casualties in a cold and heartless manner. "When an Indian gets killed," he observed, "the other Indians feel sorry and cry, and sometimes stop fighting. But when a white soldier gets killed, nobody cries, nobody cares; they go right on shooting and let him lie there. Sometimes they even go off and leave their wounded behind them."

Shortly after the Battle of Killdeer Mountain, a united army of Teton Sioux engaged Sully's troops again, this time in a rather inconclusive fight known as the Battle of the Badlands. Sometime during the long night, as the Sioux were shooting at the soldiers, a voice called out to Sitting Bull and his comrades in their own language. They learned that this voice belonged to one of the Yankton Sioux scouts, who had all become disenchanted with living among the soldiers. Sitting Bull called back to the scouts, "You have no business with the soldiers. The Indians here want no fights with white men." Then he asked them a perplexing question: "Why is it the whites come to fight with us, anyhow?" They could give no reply; soon, however, Sitting Bull would learn the answer for himself.

Emigrants Crossing the
Plains, *painted by Albert
Bierstadt in 1867. By the mid-
1860s, pioneers had set up
homesteads within 200 miles
of Hunkpapa territory. Sitting
Bull saw the influx of whites
as a threat to the Sioux way
of life.*

4

"WE WANT NO WHITE MEN HERE"

Sitting Bull's first encounters with U.S. troops taught him that there was at least as much to fear from the intrusions of the whites as there was from attacks by other Indian tribes. Indeed, by the mid-1860s, he came to view the whites as the greater threat. Although from time to time he would still engage rival tribes in battles over horses or hunting ranges, Sitting Bull's real war was now with the whites.

A steady stream of pioneers and settlers had begun to set up homesteads fewer than 200 miles east of Hunkpapa territory, and Sitting Bull feared that soon the newcomers would begin crowding the Sioux. Meanwhile, Dakota territorial governor Newton Edmunds was traveling throughout the area with a scheme to ensure peace with the Sioux. The war with the Sioux had already cost the government some $40 million. It would be cheaper, Edmunds reasoned, to pay the Sioux to keep the peace and to stop these payments if they went to war.

The "stay-around-the-fort-people," those more docile Sioux who had settled near Forts Sully and Rice, were willing to accept Edmunds's plan. However, self-sufficient Indians such as Sitting Bull rejected the payments and insisted on their right to defend themselves and their territories. Edmunds's idea was never put into practice, but his meetings with the Sioux gave him the opportunity to announce another plan — the intention of the United States government to confine all Teton people to reservations where they could be "civilized" under the supervision of federal agents.

At the same time, General Sully, from his post at Fort Rice, also attempted to make peace with the Sioux. As the Hunkpapa leaders debated Sully's offer, Sitting Bull, as war chief of the Strong Hearts, led the opposition to the truce. He was guided by a deep mistrust of everything the white men said. Sitting Bull feared that Sully wanted to get all the Indians together at Fort Rice and eliminate them in one fell swoop.

He told the others how the troops at the fort frequently fired on friendly Indians. He reminded them that at that very moment, Cheyennes and Sioux were fighting soldiers along the Platte River while more soldiers were marching into Indian hunting grounds along the Powder River. As to Sully's attempts to get the Sioux to sign lands away and to let the whites construct forts and roads in Indian territory, Sitting Bull's position was clear and concise. "We want no white men here," he declared. "The Black Hills belong to me. If the whites try to take them, I will fight."

At first, the majority of the huge Sioux camp disagreed with Sitting Bull, favoring a truce with Sully. The tide turned when a rumor spread through the camp that Sully's troops had massacred the stay-around-the-fort-people near Fort Rice. The Sioux peace party was shocked; immediately, Sitting Bull formed a war party and led 500 warriors, including those who previously had argued in favor of the truce, to the fort.

They found that the Indian camp was gone, but fortunately there had been no massacre. Apparently, Sully had begun to move troops in with the intention of

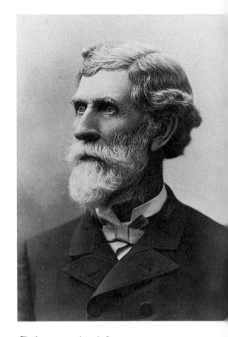

Dakota territorial governor Newton Edmunds proposed paying off Sioux Indians who kept the peace and allowed white encroachment. Sitting Bull rejected such payments and persisted in his defense of Sioux territory.

attacking these friendly Indians. However, the people were warned of the impending slaughter and had enough time to break camp and get away without a shot being fired. Recalling the Sand Creek massacre — in which troops had killed more than 130 Cheyennes, most of them women and children — Sitting Bull and the others realized that a second massacre had narrowly been averted. Here, as far as they were concerned, was proof of the value of the white man's word. There would be no truce with Sully.

In early September 1865, Sitting Bull's Sioux warriors approached the Powder River, where General Patrick Edward Connor had established a camp (later named Fort Reno). Some of the younger men, remembering Sully's peace offer, rode toward the camp in the hope that the soldiers would give them some food or tobacco. Instead, they were fired upon, and several were killed. Sitting Bull's full 400-man war party, well armed and well mounted, came into view — the army's official report overestimated their number at 3,000 — and the soldiers, approximately 1,000 of them, charged. The Sioux tactics proved extremely effective. Time and again they would allow the cavalry to chase them until the soldiers' half-starved mounts began to tire. Then, the warriors would turn and charge back at them. Many coups were counted that way, and many soldiers, but few Sioux, were killed.

Prior to the battle, Connor had issued orders to the troops "not to receive overtures of peace," but instead to "kill every male Indian over 12 years of age." Even his superior officer, General John Pope, found these orders "atrocious" and "disgraceful." Afterward, Connor wrote that as a result of the Battle of Powder River, "Harm rather than good was done, and our troops . . . were driven from their country by the Indians."

Many of Connor's troops were, from the first, unwilling to fight the Indians; some mutinied and had to be coerced by the threat of cannon fire. The night after the battle, a sudden cold snap killed their starving horses. The surviving soldiers had to burn or bury their supplies, saddles, and extra ammunition before they limped back to the camp, exhausted and discouraged. For his miserable failure in this campaign, General Connor was relieved of his command.

In 1867, Sitting Bull, then 36 years old, was inaugurated as head war chief of the Sioux. As chief, he frequently launched war parties against other Indian nations in order to secure a plentiful supply of game for his people. Sitting Bull never attacked white settlements. In fact, he cared little about the whites as long as they left the Sioux and their hunting ranges alone. He would not, however, allow the intrusions of white soldiers and settlers to destroy the buffalo supply and force his people to go hungry.

Sitting Bull's demands were simple and clear: Close the roads inside Indian Territory, raze the forts, stop the

The Attack of the Emigrant Train, *painted by Charles Wimar in 1856. Sitting Bull never attacked white settlements but tried to prevent whites from destroying the Sioux means of survival—the buffalo.*

Father Pierre Jeane De Smet, known to the Indians as Black Robe, met with Sitting Bull in 1868 to negotiate peace for the United States. After their council, De Smet gave Sitting Bull a crucifix of brass and wood, which long remained a treasured possession in the family.

steamboats, and expel all whites except traders. He was merely trying to ensure the rights that were supposed to have been guaranteed by the treaties that his nation had made with the U.S. government. Grant these conditions, he insisted, and there will be peace. However, if the security of his people was threatened, he would make war.

In June of 1868, Father Pierre Jeane De Smet, a friend of Sitting Bull's, attempted to bring peace to the Hunkpapa Sioux. Father De Smet, a Jesuit priest whom the Indians called Black Robe, had been traveling and meeting with the various Sioux tribes for the last two years. They trusted him and had become his friends. He was a genial and courageous man who sincerely wanted to help the Indians.

When he announced that he would bring his peace mission into the camp of the Hunkpapa hunters, the so-called hostile Sioux, many whites warned De Smet that this would be his most dangerous undertaking yet. However, both De Smet and his companion, Major Charles E. Galpin, a trader, were old friends of Sitting Bull's and had always dealt fairly with him.

Indeed, to their overtures of peace, Sitting Bull responded, "Tell the Black Robe we shall meet him and his friends with arms stretched out, ready to embrace him. No man living can remember that I ever treated a peace commission with contempt, or gave them hard words, or did them any harm." He even placed the priest under his personal protection because other Hunkpapas were suspicious and intended to kill De Smet and his party once they entered the camp.

Sitting Bull told De Smet of his deep desire for peace. "Black Robe," he implored him, "I hardly sustain myself beneath the weight of white men's blood that I have shed. The whites provoked the war. . . . I will listen to your good words. And as bad as I have been to the white men, just so good I am ready to become toward them."

Black Robe told him of the planned treaty. "Your Grandfather [the president] wishes you to live among your people on your own lands," De Smet insisted. "You will never starve. You will always have plenty of rations. You will not be captives, but at liberty."

Sitting Bull answered that he had a message for the Grandfather. "I myself have plans for my people," he explained, "and if they follow my plans they will never want. They will never hunger. I wish for traders only, and no soldiers on my reservation. . . . We can live if we keep our Black Hills. We do not want to eat from the hand of the Grandfather. We can feed ourselves."

The next day the great peace council met. First De Smet addressed the assembled chiefs and warriors, exhorting them that for the sake of their people and their children, they must listen to and accept his offering of peace. Black Moon, an important Hunkpapa leader and a renowned orator, then spoke, enumerating the Sioux's many grievances against the whites. He closed with the simple, and hopeful, phrase, "Let the past be forgotten."

Now it was Sitting Bull's turn to address the assembly. He spoke eloquently, blaming the whites for the past wars but assuring De Smet that he hoped he might "for all time to come remain a friend of the whites." He ended his speech, shook hands with De Smet and Galpin, and sat down to thunderous applause. Then, he arose again, saying that he had "forgotten two things" — his conditions for the treaty. First, Sitting Bull asserted, "I do not propose to sell any part of my country." Second, he insisted, "those forts filled with white soldiers must be abandoned." These were his terms of peace.

After the council ended, a delegation of Hunkpapas went with De Smet back to Fort Rice. Sitting Bull was

Gall, photographed by David F. Barry, traveled with Bull Owl to Fort Rice in 1868 to sign the Treaty of Laramie on behalf of the Hunkpapa Sioux.

not among them; he refused to go and in his place sent a Hunkpapa leader known as Gall. On July 2, 1868, Gall and Bull Owl, on behalf of the Hunkpapa Sioux, signed the Treaty of Laramie.

This new treaty established the Great Sioux Reservation in the Dakota Territory west of the Missouri River and north of the Dakota-Nebraska border. It provided that "no white person shall be permitted to settle upon or occupy any portion" of this Indian territory, or to pass through it without first having obtained the consent of the Indians. The military posts on the Bozeman Trail

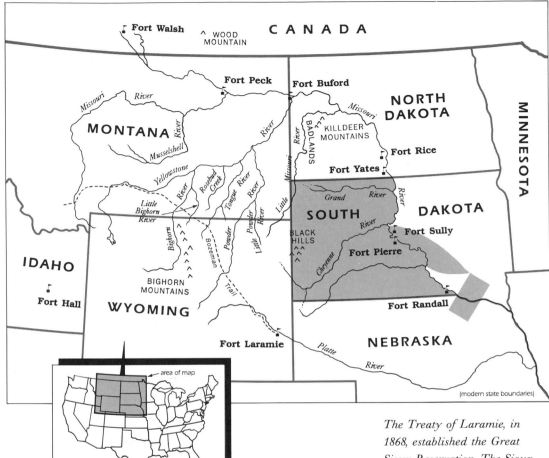

The Treaty of Laramie, in 1868, established the Great Sioux Reservation. The Sioux could legally hunt on any land north of the Platte River "so long as buffalo may range thereon in such numbers to justify the chase."

were abandoned and the trail itself was closed. Finally, the treaty stipulated that no future treaty would be valid unless it was signed by three-fourths of the adult males of the tribe. The only demand made of the Sioux was that they keep the peace. At least on paper, the treaty was a complete victory for the Sioux and testimony to Sitting Bull's political skill.

As long as the boundaries established by the Treaty of Laramie in 1868 were not violated, Sitting Bull continued to keep his distance from the whites. However, he dealt severely with those whom he caught illegally within the Sioux hunting grounds. Sometimes they got away with a warning. More often, they paid for their transgression with their horses, supplies, weapons, and clothes. If a foolish adventurer tried to resist capture, he most likely would be killed.

In January 1869, a party led by Sitting Bull encountered a lone mail courier on the trail between Forts Hall and Peck. He was captured and nearly killed by two of the band, until Sitting Bull saw his face. The man, Frank Grouard, was the son of a white sailor and a woman from the Sandwich Islands in the South Pacific; his mother's ethnic background gave Grouard a complexion similar to that of an Indian. Sitting Bull ordered the others to let him go.

When they returned to camp, Grouard feared the worst. But then Sitting Bull announced that, as he had done years earlier with the Assiniboin boy now known as Jumping Bull, he was adopting the mail courier into his family. He named his new brother Sitting-with-Upraised-Hands (or Hands Up); this was a reference to a bear, inspired by the bearskin coat Grouard was wearing when he was captured. Grouard was well treated by the Hunkpapa and stayed in the camp for three years. However, unlike the chief's other adopted brother, a brave warrior and an ever-loyal comrade to Sitting Bull, Grouard would turn his back on his adopted people and become a scout for the U.S. Army.

For the next several years, Sitting Bull was occupied with defending the Sioux hunting grounds from incursions by other Indian nations. In the winter of 1869, he led his warriors in a particularly fierce battle with their longtime enemies, the Crows. Thirty Crows were killed that day, as Sitting Bull personally counted three coups. His brother, Jumping Bull, by then a sash-wearer of the Strong Hearts, fought valiantly as well. But victory came at a high price for the Hunkpapa warriors; 14 of them were killed, including Sitting Bull's youngest uncle, Looks-for-Home, and 18 were wounded.

Not long after this battle with the Crows, a great number of Sioux had assembled along the Yellowstone River at the mouth of the Powder River. The camp numbered almost 1,000 lodges and included Hunkpapa, Oglala, Minneconjou, and Sans-Arc Sioux. The summer hunting season was over, and the warriors, especially the younger men, were eager for battle and the glory and honors that it might bring them. A war party of 400 assembled and headed north. While the scouts were out looking for enemy camps, some of the impatient warriors asked Sitting Bull, whose powers of prophecy were highly regarded, to see if he could divine what was going to happen. He said he would try, and he walked away from the crowd, singing.

When he returned he lighted his pipe and told them that in the smoke he could see a battle within two days. In it, he prophesied, many enemies and several Sioux would be killed. Then he added that while he was singing, he saw a spark coming toward him. They all knew what this sign meant; Sitting Bull himself would be injured in the battle.

The scouts returned to report a Flathead camp on the Musselshell River. Sitting Bull announced that he had a plan. He proposed that a small party of young men on fast horses ride down to engage the enemy. The older warriors would stay behind, out of sight. When the Flatheads saw how few of the Sioux there were, they would chase them. Then the young men could lead the enemy into an ambush.

Everyone agreed to Sitting Bull's scheme. It was both good military strategy and good politics. Old and young warriors often were jealous of each other; Sitting Bull's plan gave them both an important role in the battle. The

Frank Grouard, though caught trespassing in Sioux territory, escaped the wrath of Sitting Bull and became his adopted brother. Unlike Jumping Bull, he would prove to be disloyal to his adopted people.

young men could ride ahead, as they probably would anyway. But the older men also would have ample opportunity to distinguish themselves in the fighting and share in the glory. Most importantly, both factions would have to work together, thus ensuring victory.

The plan worked perfectly and the Flatheads were routed. However, Sitting Bull's prophecy was all too accurate. Near the end of the battle, he was shot through the forearm by an enemy arrow. The wound was severe, but it was well cared for and soon healed. In his victory over the Flatheads, Sitting Bull displayed, as he had so many times before, both the strategic mind and the courageous heart of a great leader.

Sitting Bull spent the summer of 1872 again fighting the Crows. By the end of the summer, however, it was the whites who once more posed the greater threat. Colonel D. S. Stanley was in command of a military escort accompanying a survey party of the Northern Pacific Railroad. The survey, which placed the railroad on the south bank of the river, was a violation of the 1868 treaty. It was the army's job to secure this territory on behalf of this new and powerful enterprise, the railroad. In other words, the soldiers were not carrying out a military mission, but an economic one. Stanley's troops repeatedly skirmished with Indians, some of whom were under the leadership of Hunkpapa chief Gall.

Gall reported back to Sitting Bull that soldiers were coming up the Yellowstone. The Sioux war chief organized a large party of Hunkpapas, Oglalas, Minneconjous, Sans-Arcs, Blackfoot Sioux, and Cheyennes to meet the troops and attempt to warn them off. "They have no business in our country," he insisted. At daybreak on the morning of August 14, Sitting Bull's band reached the soldiers' camp in the valley of the Yellowstone River. There was no chance to talk, however; the soldiers, 400 of them, including 182 cavalrymen, came out fighting. The battle raged on all morning.

A medicine man named Long Holy had recently organized a kind of cult consisting of seven young warriors. According to instructions that he had received in a vision, he made them believe they were bulletproof. This battle, he felt, provided a perfect opportunity to display his power. His protégés circled recklessly toward the soldiers, who, of course, fired at them. By the time they completed their second circle, four of them had been hit, although none were killed.

As the young warriors were beginning their third circle toward the troops, Sitting Bull galloped in to stop their foolhardy display. "Too many young men are being wounded!" he shouted. "That's enough!" By exposing

A drawing made by Sitting Bull depicting his battle with a Flathead. Before the encounter, the chief prophesied correctly that the Flatheads would be routed and that he himself would suffer an injury.

themselves in front of the soldiers' lines, the young men already had shown their courage. There was, the chief felt, no point in having them all killed.

Sitting Bull persuaded them to stop, but then Long Holy cast some aspersions on the chief's courage. Clearly, the war chief of all the Sioux could not afford to ignore these remarks. So, he walked out toward the soldiers, sat down on the open prairie, and leisurely smoked his pipe. He called to his astonished warriors, "Any Indians who wish to smoke with me, come on!" He was joined by four others. Only when he had finished his tobacco and scraped out the bowl of the pipe did he stroll back to the main group. The others ran back in great haste.

Although Sitting Bull's exhibition did not help bring about an Indian victory that day, it was a great boost for his warriors' morale. It reminded the Sioux of the great bravery of their nation — and their leader. None of them had ever seen anything like it. It was not a coup, but it was braver than any coup ever counted.

The battle ended around noon with neither side victorious. Really, it was no more than a show of force, a demonstration to the white soldiers that the Indians would not tolerate any invasion of their territory in violation of the treaty. Sitting Bull still did not consider himself to be at war with the whites. He discussed the matter with his friend and adviser Crazy Horse, who said to him, "My friend, if any soldiers or white men come in here and do not shoot first, we'll not bother them. But if they come shooting, we'll go after them." Sitting Bull agreed, and thereafter that would be his policy: If they come shooting, shoot back.

5

▼▼▼

DEFENDING THE NEST

For many years it was rumored that the Black Hills of the Dakota Territory were filled with gold. As early as 1872, hopeful prospectors began to enter the hills in greater and greater numbers. In the summer of 1874, the government sent an expedition into the hills to assess the real value of the gold deposits.

Although this was termed a "scientific mission," the small number of scientists was guarded heavily by a menacing military escort — 10 companies of the Seventh Cavalry, 2 companies of infantry, 60 scouts, 4 Gatling guns, and a long wagon train loaded with supplies. The expedition was commanded by George Armstrong Custer.

The deployment of such a formidable military force would indicate that the government, not without good reason, expected trouble from the local Indians. The Custer expedition, and a second one led by Colonel Richard Dodge in the spring of 1875, clearly violated the Treaty of Laramie and aroused the ire of the Sioux. Indeed, Custer's supply wagons dug a trail into the heart of the Black Hills that Sitting Bull's people resentfully dubbed the Thieves' Road. Still, the expeditions encountered no hostile opposition from the Indians.

Custer and Dodge both knew that negative reports would discourage further illegal entries into the Indians'

George Custer, shown here in a major general's uniform, led the Seventh Cavalry and a group of scientists through the heart of the Black Hills in 1874 without the consent of the Sioux.

Custer's expedition, including soldiers, scouts, Gatling guns, and a long train of supply wagons, left behind a trail that the Sioux resentfully called Thieves' Road.

territory and keep the peace. On the other hand, claims of substantial and numerous gold deposits would bring on a rush of prospectors and set the stage for violent confrontations with the rightful occupants, the Sioux. Although the expeditions did locate a little gold, their reports wildly inflated these modest findings. Custer, for example, declared that he had found gold in the grass roots. Word spread quickly, and a gold rush began in the Black Hills.

The army was supposed to check the flood of prospectors into Sioux land. However, its performance of this duty was, at best, half-hearted. General Philip H. Sheridan, for example, complained that having to police whites on behalf of the Indians was a "most embarrassing duty." So, while the army sat on its hands, more than 1,000 prospectors invaded the Black Hills. These rugged opportunists pressured the government to buy the mining rights from the Sioux. A commission was dispatched from Washington to the Great Sioux Reservation. Its job was to convince the Sioux to give up a piece of land that, according to the Treaty of Laramie, was supposed to have been theirs forever.

The Sioux, however, refused to sell these rights. Then the government offered Red Cloud, one of the most pliable and conciliatory of all the Sioux chiefs, $6 million to purchase the land outright. To the commission's surprise, Red Cloud rejected the government's offer and demanded $70 million. Not surprisingly, Sitting Bull was even less compromising; he declined to meet with the commission and refused to sell the Black Hills at any price. Crazy Horse agreed. "One does not sell the earth upon which the people walk," he grumbled.

The commissioners returned to Washington and reported their failure. They then recommended that the government simply disregard the wishes of the Indians and set a "reasonable" price for the Black Hills and offer it to the Sioux as an ultimatum. The government's failure to enforce the Treaty of Laramie, followed by its heavy-handed attempt to extract a forced purchase of the Black Hills, set the stage for all-out war between the Sioux and the U.S. Army.

On December 3, 1875, at the request of President Ulysses S. Grant, Secretary of the Interior Zachariah Chandler wrote to Secretary of War William Belknap that he had directed the commissioner of Indian affairs to notify all Sioux and Cheyennes living outside the reservations that "they must remove to a reservation before the 31st day of January next." If they did not do so, "they [would] be reported to the War Department as hostile Indians, and . . . a military force [would] be sent to compel them to obey the orders."

Unlike Red Cloud, who was known as an "agency Indian" because he had chosen to settle his people on a reservation under the direction of an agent of the U.S. government, Sitting Bull could not confine himself to a reservation. To him, the entire Dakota Territory, the Great Sioux Reservation as specified in the Treaty of Laramie, was his "agency." Finding the government's order both unreasonable and arrogant, Sitting Bull simply did not comply. Even if he had wanted to lead his people to the agency, the extremely harsh weather that winter would have prevented him. Furthermore, he knew that there was nothing to eat at the agency; his own camp was full of starving agency Indians who had left the reservation to hunt with him.

In any event, Sitting Bull remained at large. On February 1, 1876, the secretary of the interior sent another letter to the secretary of war. He wrote that because Sitting Bull still refused to comply with the directions of the commissioner of Indian affairs, Sitting Bull and his people would hereby be turned over to the War Department "for such action on the part of the Army" as the secretary of war deemed "proper under the circumstances." Six days later, the War Department authorized operations against the "hostile Sioux," specifically the bands under the leadership of Crazy Horse and Sitting Bull. In short, the United States government had declared war on the Sioux.

In March, General George Crook set out after Crazy Horse's Oglala camp, which was reported to be a few miles above the mouth of the Little Powder River in the present-day state of Montana. Although some Oglalas were there, this was, in fact, the camp of the Cheyenne chief Two Moon; Crazy Horse was actually camped miles away. The troops were led to the peaceful Cheyenne village by Frank Grouard, Sitting Bull's adopted brother who had become an army scout. They attacked, but encountered fierce resistance and were driven back. Nevertheless, the Indians were forced to abandon their camp, which the soldiers burned. And so, the Cheyennes were drawn into the war.

Two Moon brought his people to the camp of Crazy Horse, and the two chiefs dedicated themselves to fighting the white man. Then they led the camps to the village of their friend and ally, Sitting Bull. He welcomed the refugee Cheyennes and Oglalas warmly, giving them food, horses, saddles, robes, ammunition, and a place to stay. When he heard their story, Sitting Bull grew angry; his patience with the whites finally was at an end. "We are an island of Indians in a lake of whites," he said bitterly. "We must stand together, or they will rub us out separately. These soldiers have come shooting; they want war. All right, we'll give it to them!"

Runners sped from Sitting Bull's camp to every Sioux, Cheyenne, and Arapaho hunting camp and agency west of the Missouri River, calling them to join Sitting Bull at the bend of the Rosebud River for one big fight with the soldiers. The response was overwhelming. During the spring of 1876, the trails in the northern prairie were filled with people, all of them heading for Sitting Bull's camp. Along with Sitting Bull's Hunkpapas, there were Oglalas, Minneconjous, Sans-Arcs, and Cheyennes in great numbers, as well as many Brules and Arapahos, and some Yanktonais, Two-Kettles, Blackfoot Sioux, and Santees.

Once the size of the camp had reached around 300 lodges, Sitting Bull called the various chiefs together for a war council. Two Moon was elected to lead the Cheyennes in the war, and, naturally, Sitting Bull was chosen unanimously to command the Sioux. Then Sitting

Bull set about making preparations for the upcoming fight. He sent out young men to rustle all the horses they could and told them, "Spare nobody. If you meet anyone, kill him, and take his horse. Let no one live."

The inevitable approach of battle colored Sitting Bull's personality. Now that he had dedicated himself completely to the cause of war, he seemed, to some observers, ruthless, almost callous. A handful of Sioux and Cheyennes even considered going back to the agencies, but the warrior societies that policed the camp would not allow it. Young Two Moon, the nephew of the Cheyenne chief whose name he shared, recalled that "Sitting Bull was a goodhearted man to his own people. But he was a mean warrior; he loved to kill. . . . In those days only one thing smelled good to him — gunpowder." But given the task that lay ahead, Sitting Bull's behavior was not really so strange. He was a general preparing for war, and he acted like one.

A pictograph of Sitting Bull counting coup on a white man who is covered with body hair, a characteristic considered loathsome to the Sioux. Once Sitting Bull decided he had no choice but to fight the whites, he declared, "Let no one live."

The Plains Indians rarely gathered in large numbers. The difficulties of obtaining a sufficient supply of food for themselves and their pony herds generally prevented the creation of large communities. However, since ancient times, they had shown, when necessary, the ability to band and work together in great numbers, particularly during periods of warfare. None of the U.S. military commanders, not even Custer, one of the most experienced Indian fighters in the army, expected to encounter unified opposition from such a large concentration of Indians.

By early June, this huge assembly of Sioux and Cheyennes began moving toward the Little Bighorn River and the land they called the valley of the Greasy Grass, in present-day southern Montana; they were motivated by the most powerful factor known — the survival of their way of life.

The previous autumn, Sitting Bull had made a sacred vow to the Sioux god, Wakan' Tanka, that he would give him a "scarlet blanket" the following summer. The time had now arrived for him to fulfill that pledge and perform the elaborate Sun Dance ritual. That scarlet blanket would be his own blood.

In the Sun Dance ritual, the subject would bleed himself and then dance, gazing at the sun, until he dropped. The combination of pain and exhaustion caused him to experience visions and prophecies, what modern medicine would call hallucinations. The Sioux, a mystical people, gave great significance to these visions. Because of the seriousness of the task that lay ahead, Sitting Bull decided to offer 100 pieces of flesh — 50 bits of skin to be cut from each arm.

With a sharp steel awl and a scalpel, Jumping Bull began cutting the small pieces of skin from his brother, Sitting Bull. Soon both of the chief's arms were covered in a scarlet blanket of blood. All the while, Sitting Bull remained perfectly still, never wincing in pain, but wailing in prayer to Wakan' Tanka. The agonizing ordeal lasted about half an hour.

Then Sitting Bull began his sun-gazing dance. He danced all day and through the night until, at about noon the next day, the crowd noticed that he was nearly unconscious and barely able to stand. Some of the observers took him and laid him down. After they dowsed him with cold water to revive him, Sitting Bull spoke softly to his friend and fellow chief, Black Moon. He had experienced a vision.

Black Moon declared loudly, "Sitting Bull wishes to announce that he just heard a voice from above saying, *'I give you these because they have no ears.'* He looked up and saw soldiers and some Indians on horseback coming down like grasshoppers. . . . They were falling right into our camp." The Sun Dance ritual was brought to an end; it was June 14, 1876.

The camp was overjoyed and filled with a fighting spirit. Through their chief, Sitting Bull, Wakan' Tanka had assured his people that he would take care of them. The white men who had "no ears," that is, who would not listen, and who had made war on the Indians, would be killed. Sitting Bull's prediction of doom for the troops proved to be his most powerful prophecy. Indeed, 10 days later, when the Ree Indian scouts who served Custer's troops heard of the ceremony, they warned the reckless general, "The Sioux are sure of winning."

By mid-June, Sitting Bull's camp had relocated to Reno (or Ash) Creek, between the Rosebud and the Little Bighorn rivers. Between 12,000 and 15,000 tipis, housing 4,000 to 5,000 warriors and their families, stretched for 3 miles along the Little Bighorn — one of the largest concentrations of Indians to ever gather on the Plains. General George Crook, whom the Indians named Three

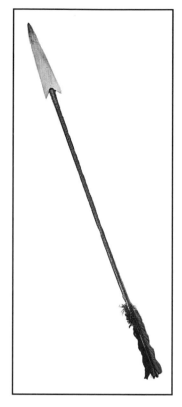

An arrow used for cutting flesh during the Sun Dance ritual. Sitting Bull offered 100 pieces of his own skin in this ritual to the Sioux god Wakan' Tanka before fighting in the Battle of the Rosebud in June 1876.

Stars for his general's insignia, and a force of more than 1,000 soldiers as well as 260 Crow, Shoshone, and Ree scouts, were stationed at the headwaters of the Rosebud.

On the morning of June 17, a great war party of 1,000 warriors attacked Three Stars's camp. Because the Sun Dance, completed just three days earlier, had taken a great deal out of Sitting Bull, the campaign was directed by Crazy Horse. But Sitting Bull nevertheless took part in the battle — he would not miss this opportunity to strike a heavy blow against the soldiers.

General George Crook, known to the Indians as Three Stars, had no choice but to retreat after losing the Battle of the Rosebud. Several months later, he would return to attack the Sioux at Slim Buttes.

The battle lasted six hours, and when it was over, General Crook had learned a great deal about the fighting ability of the Plains Indians. With nearly 100 soldiers dead or wounded, and his ammunition severely depleted, Crook had no choice but to order a retreat. The Battle of the Rosebud was the most decisive victory yet for the Indians over the U.S. Army. Still, they realized that Sitting Bull's prophecy had not been fulfilled. He had predicted that the soldiers would fall right into their camp, but Three Stars' men were killed some 20 miles away.

After the battle, Sitting Bull and the other chiefs decided to return the camp to the valley of the Greasy Grass, on the Little Bighorn River. Scouts had reported that great herds of antelope were there and that grass for the horses was plentiful. Once they arrived at the new campground, the Indians rested, hunted, danced, tended to their horses, cared for the wounded, buried the dead, and in general, took care of the needs of daily life. No one was frightened or apprehensive about the future. The Battle of the Rosebud had proved that they could fight the white soldiers and beat them. Although they made no offensive plans, the Indians were ready to fight if the troops attacked. In Sitting Bull's words, "Even a bird will defend its nest."

By this time, the U.S. Army had mobilized a force of about 2,500 for its intended attack on the Sioux-Cheyenne encampment. The plan was for Custer's Seventh Cavalry, which his commander, General Alfred Terry, considered his most effective tactical force, to proceed up the Rosebud and trap the Sioux between the remaining two forces of troops. The attack was originally set for the morning of June 26. However, Custer was worried that the Sioux might escape. So, to push the battle forward by one day, he marched his men on the night of June 24, under cover of darkness, to about 10 miles from the Little Bighorn.

General George Armstrong Custer, known to the Indians as Long Hair because of his distinctive long locks, first achieved fame as "the boy general" of the Civil War. His division had led the pursuit of the Confederate commander, General Robert E. Lee, and it was to Custer that the Confederates brought their white flag just before Lee's final surrender at Appomattox in 1865. Regarding Custer's role in the Union victory, his superior, General Philip H. Sheridan, reported, "I know of no one whose efforts have contributed more to this happy result than those of Custer."

Custer was notorious among the military for both his recklessness and his good fortune; "Custer's luck" was a well-worn expression within the officer corps. He was also strong willed and independent to the point of arrogance. He had broken with the corrupt and incompetent administration of President Ulysses S. Grant, the hero of the Civil War. Indeed, his criticisms of Grant almost cost Custer the command of the Seventh Cavalry.

Custer was also politically ambitious. With the 1876 presidential elections fewer than five months away, he was convinced that a major victory over the Indians could secure for him the Democratic party's nomination. After all, Custer reasoned, the American people had a tradition of elevating their military heroes to the White House. Grant, Zachary Taylor (the 12th president), William Henry Harrison (the ninth president), and of course George Washington, all had ascended to the presidency directly by way of their victories on the battlefield. In a few short months, he could be President George Armstrong Custer — at 37, the youngest man ever elected to the office.

The evening before his fateful encounter with Sitting Bull's legions, Custer confided in his Ree scouts. He told the Rees that he was counting on them to help him win; if he did, he soon would be "the Grandfather," the president, and he would use his power to reward them

Custer posing with his Ree scouts, whom he counted on to help him defeat the Sioux. After hearing about Sitting Bull's Sun Dance, the scouts warned Custer that the Sioux were sure of defeating him.

for their help and their loyalty. The Rees were not so sure. They kept telling the general that he would find more Sioux and Cheyennes in the valley of the Greasy Grass than he could handle. However, hungry for battle and ambitious for power, Custer did not listen to them. He was certain that once he found the Indians, they would be running from him.

Upon his troops' arrival at the Little Bighorn, Custer split his 650 officers and men into 3 battalions, one under his command, one under Major Frederick Benteen, and one under Major Marcus Reno. Reno's troops were to attack the upper end of the camp first, tying up as many Indian warriors as possible so that Custer could strike at the camp's lower end. The campaign was a disaster from the start.

On the morning of June 25, 1876, Reno's men assaulted the Sioux-Cheyenne village at the Hunkpapa encampment. Amid the confusion brought on by this sudden onslaught of troops, Sitting Bull and Gall organized the Indians' resistance. The women and children were moved in great haste downstream to safety, and the warriors mounted their horses and rode out to meet the soldiers.

As more and more reinforcements joined the Sioux forces, the troops were stopped in their tracks. Suddenly, and to the Indians' great surprise, the soldiers got off their horses and attempted to fight on foot. The Indians charged, driving Reno's men back toward the woods. This hasty retreat quickly turned into a rout. The Sioux descended upon the soldiers with bullets, arrows, and clubs, killing more than 30 of them.

At first, Sitting Bull was puzzled by Reno's behavior. Why did he attack with just a handful of men? And then, why did he have his men dismount and attempt to fight on foot? But Sitting Bull, a skilled and cunning military tactician, soon realized the answer — Reno had fought on foot and taken cover in the trees because he was waiting for help. There must be, Sitting Bull reasoned, another party of soldiers ready to attack. He urged his warriors to be cautious.

Many historians of the Battle of Little Bighorn have criticized Reno, inexperienced in Indian warfare, for poor leadership. Some have even accused him of extreme cowardice. In his retreat, they say, he deserted his superior, Custer, leaving him at the mercy of the enemy. Others, however, have argued that Reno was badly outnumbered; observers on both sides estimated that he faced between 900 and 1,000 warriors. According to his defenders, Reno, surrounded after his initial, ill-fated charge, had little choice but to retreat and wait for reinforcements from Benteen. However, they arrived too late to be of any help.

In any event, Sitting Bull was correct about the army's strategy. There was a second force waiting to attack — Custer's five companies to the east. Having repelled the soldiers' first assault, Gall was able to divert hundreds of his warriors to a frontal attack on Custer. Crazy Horse and Two Moon struck Custer's flank and rear.

Concerned that Reno might regroup and attempt a second attack on the camp, Sitting Bull stayed behind to protect the women and children. If Benteen's men had not been delayed, there certainly would have been another assault on the village. Although Sitting Bull did not take part in the actual fighting against Custer's forces, his skill in predicting the enemy's plans and movements contributed enormously to the Indians' victory on that fateful day.

In their pursuit of Custer's forces, the Sioux and Cheyennes initially had the soldiers at a great disadvantage, pulling them off their horses and capturing their mounts, guns, and ammunition. Once the soldiers dis-

mounted, however, their superior firepower temporarily gave them the edge. For a brief time, the troops shot the mounted Indians out of their saddles. But as the battle proceeded, the Indians were able to capture many of the soldiers' horses and found pistols and bullets in the saddlebags. This finally turned the tide against Custer's men, and as the number of soldiers decreased, the Indians rushed in to fight them hand-to-hand.

With their ranks quickly diminishing, the remaining soldiers had little chance against these experts in the art of single combat. When Custer made his famous "last stand" there were only about 20 of his men left standing. At the end of the battle, Long Hair, the great Indian fighter, the man who had cut the hated Thieves' Road and had opened up the Black Hills to white settlement, was dead. Scattered around him were the bodies of his entire battalion, all 225 of them. About 30 Indians died in the fighting that day.

A lithograph of S. H. Redmond's drawing General Custer's Death Struggle. The Battle of the Little Big Horn. *Custer and his whole battalion were wiped out at Little Bighorn. The night after the battle, Sitting Bull grieved for all who had died.*

By evening, Benteen's men finally arrived to reinforce Reno's badly beaten forces, who were dug in downriver. The Indians surrounded them, firing until it got too dark. The following morning, the shooting resumed, and when it was over, 18 more white men had been killed.

On the night of the Battle of Little Bighorn, Sitting Bull grieved for the dead, Custer's as well as his own. "Tonight," he commanded, "we shall mourn for our dead, and for those brave white men lying up yonder on the hillside."

He was sad for another reason as well. Against his warnings, many of the young warriors had carried off souvenirs from the battlefield — guns, horses, clothing. "Because you have taken the spoils," Sitting Bull lamented, "henceforth you will covet the white man's goods, you will be at his mercy, you will starve at his hands." His words were to prove tragically prophetic in the years to come.

As the Indians were fighting Reno's soldiers the second time, scouts returned to the camp with news that many more soldiers were marching toward the Little Bighorn. A council convened, and the Indians decided to break camp. As the sun began to set, they started upriver toward the Bighorn Mountains. There they held their victory dance.

The camp stayed together until early August, but it finally became too difficult to find enough meat for such a huge gathering. By summer's end, the various tribal groups had split up and gone their separate directions. The combined forces of Plains Indians had beaten the U.S. Army in the first battle of the Great Sioux War. Sitting Bull must have been elated to have commanded such a powerful and successful legion; however, to the misfortune of him and his people, that elation would not last very long.

The Sioux Indian commission that convinced a few agency chiefs to sign away the Black Hills in the Treaty of 1876.

6

"THEY ARE ALL LIARS"

News of Custer's defeat at the Battle of Little Bighorn quickly reached the East. The politicians in Washington called it a "massacre." In retaliation, the government sought to punish every Indian it could find, even those who had remained on the reservations and took no part in the fighting. On July 22, 1876, General William Tecumseh Sherman was given the authority to place the reservations under military control and treat the inhabitants as prisoners of war.

In mid-August, Congress, maintaining that the Indians had violated the 1868 treaty by going to war against the United States, passed a law requiring the Indians to give up all rights to the Black Hills and the Powder River country. Of course, the lawmakers had overlooked the fact that it was the U.S. Army that had invaded the Indians' territory and launched the first assaults. The new law provided that no rations be supplied to the Indians at the agencies until they relinquished all claims to these lands. In effect, the government intended to starve the Sioux into giving up the land to which, by tradition and treaty, they were entitled.

A commission was sent from Washington to convince and, if necessary, threaten the agency chiefs into signing away their land. At first, the chiefs, such as Red Cloud and Spotted Tail, argued that they could do nothing at that time. They reminded the commissioners that the 1868 treaty required the signatures of three-quarters of all the adult males; more than half of the warriors, however, were in the north with Sitting Bull and Crazy Horse. The commissioners responded that the Indians who went off the reservation were hostile. The treaty, they insisted, covered only "friendly" Indians, the Indians who remained on the reservation.

The chiefs had been argued into a corner by the commissioners. They were presented with a horrible choice — sign away their people's birthright or allow them to starve. Disgusted, yet humbled, they all signed. The Black Hills were gone — stolen.

Nevertheless, the government realized that so-called hostiles like Sitting Bull would not give up their land so easily; only military force could make them submit. Indeed, there was a rapid and huge buildup in the size and strength of cavalry regiments in the northern Plains. By the fall of 1876, the field commanders in the area had at their disposal almost 50 percent of the total officers and men of the entire U.S. Army.

Driven by revenge, the army prowled the Plains, killing Indians wherever they found them. On the morning of September 9, an alarm rang through Sitting Bull's village: people were being killed at the camp of American Horse (also known as Iron Shield) near Slim Buttes. The chief quickly prepared for battle; he and nearly 1,000 warriors rode off to the village, 30 miles away. Along the way they met refugees who filled in the details for them. Before light, they reported bitterly, about 150 to 200 soldiers had launched a vicious attack, killing children, women, and old people indiscriminately.

By the time Sitting Bull and his men arrived, 2,000 troops under the command of General Crook, or Three Stars, had joined the assault. Only a few months before,

Red Cloud, shown here in an 1880 photograph by Charles M. Bell, signed the Treaty of 1876. The whites considered him a "friendly" Indian.

Sitting Bull's warriors had routed Three Stars at the Battle of the Rosebud. Crook's scout was Frank Grouard. Sitting Bull's treacherous "brother" was repaying the chief's mercy by helping the army to kill his people. Sitting Bull and his warriors, outnumbered two to one, kept fighting all afternoon. This time, however, Three Stars's forces, better armed and more numerous, were able to hold them off until dark. The fighting resumed briefly the next day, but Crook marched his troops into the Black Hills and got away.

Once the soldiers were gone, Sitting Bull entered the village. American Horse, the chief, was dead. Sitting Bull saw the bodies of the victims and listened to the survivors' tales. Compared to this event, what happened in the valley of the Greasy Grass, when his army fought and defeated Custer's men, was no massacre, but rather a fierce battle between two forces of armed warriors. This attack, however, was unprovoked, perpetuated upon helpless people by the army of the United States — a real massacre.

The army's campaign against the Sioux and Cheyennes during the fall and winter of 1876 prompted many dispirited and broken warriors to surrender at the agencies. By October, even Sitting Bull was left with only a few chiefs and no more than 1,000 of the most determined holdouts. Hoping to get as far away from the soldiers as possible, Sitting Bull led his followers north along the Yellowstone River to a place where they could hunt buffalo.

They had not traveled far enough, however. Colonel Nelson A. Miles and his troops had reached the Yellowstone at about the same time as Sitting Bull. Miles was commanding the construction of a new fort to be located where the Tongue River flowed into the Yellowstone — Fort Keogh, named for Captain Myles Keogh, one of the casualties at Little Bighorn.

A group of Sitting Bull's warriors, under Gall's leadership, discovered a wagon train bringing supplies to the new fort. They attacked, made off with 47 army mules, and forced the train to turn back. Shortly after, a party of 8 men, including Sitting Bull's nephew, White Bull, encountered another wagon train, this time surrounded by 200 soldiers on foot. The Indians skirmished with the infantrymen, and White Bull was shot and wounded, although not critically.

Sitting Bull enlisted Johnny Brughière, a part Indian who had joined his camp, to write a note in English to the commander of the soldiers. It was posted on a stick in plain sight:

> YELLOWSTONE
> I want to know what you are doing on this road. You scare all the buffalo away. I want to hunt in this place. I want you to turn back from here. If you don't, I will fight you again. I want you to leave what you have got here and turn back from here.
> I am your friend
> *Sitting Bull*
> I mean all the rations you have got and some powder.
> Wish you would write as soon as you can.

The officer in charge of the wagon train, Colonel Elwell Otis, discovered this message, and sent a scout with his reply. The soldiers were going to Fort Keogh, he said, and many more would be joining them. If Sitting Bull wanted a fight, they would give him one.

Sitting Bull did not want a fight, though. All he wanted was to be left alone so that he and his people could hunt buffalo. He sent a warrior under the white flag of truce with an offer to meet with the soldiers' commander on the open prairie. By this time, Colonel Miles and his troops had overtaken the train. Miles had been searching for Sitting Bull since the end of the summer and readily

Johnny Brughière, on fleeing a murder charge, came to Sitting Bull's camp, where he was adopted by the chief and served the Sioux as an interpreter. Later, Colonel Nelson Miles cleared him of the charge and enlisted him as a scout against Sitting Bull.

agreed to the meeting.

Miles and Sitting Bull held their first meeting on October 22, seated on the prairie between a line of Sioux warriors and a line of U.S. soldiers. Because the day was very cold, Miles wore a long coat trimmed with bear fur. From that point on, the Indians called him Bear Coat. Miles recalled Sitting Bull as "a strong, hardy, sturdy looking man." He appeared, in the colonel's view, "very deliberate in his movements and somewhat reserved in his manners," and his demeanor "was civil and to some extent one of calm repose."

At the start of the meeting, Miles interrogated Sitting Bull about his supposed hostility toward whites. Sitting Bull replied that he never was against white men, and did not want to fight them if he did not have to. "All I am looking out for," he explained, "is to see how and where I can find more meat for my people . . . to find what God has given me to eat." Then, Bear Coat mentioned going to the reservation, but Sitting Bull rejected the suggestion. He and his people, he insisted, would spend the winter in the Black Hills. The meeting was cordial, but nothing was resolved. Sitting Bull and Miles agreed to meet again the next day.

This second meeting was far less friendly. Sitting Bull repeated his well-known demands to Bear Coat — remove the military posts from these hunting grounds, and clear the Black Hills of all whites. The session grew increasingly heated; Miles was not about to talk Sitting Bull out of a lifelong policy in a 15-minute meeting. White Bull arrived to calm down Sitting Bull, and to tell him that the soldiers appeared to be getting ready for battle.

At that point, Sitting Bull abruptly ended the proceedings. "Now let the talk be over," he announced to Miles. "You are losing your temper. Your soldiers are preparing to fight us again." Sitting Bull rejoined his line, and the soldiers did indeed open fire. One Indian died in the clash. The fighting continued the next day, but the Sioux were able to get away without further casualties.

Sitting Bull spent the winter moving up and down the Yellowstone from the Bighorn Mountains to the Powder River. Twice his people were struck by the troops, and although no Sioux were killed, they lost 60 horses and mules. Throughout these months, Sitting Bull searched for his friend Crazy Horse, but the Oglala warrior was nowhere to be found. The weather was bitter; the people had great trouble finding meat. In the spring of 1877, Sitting Bull brought his weary and shrinking band, about 135 lodges in all, across the northern border into the land of the Grandmother (Queen Victoria) — Canada.

Just after the victory at the Little Bighorn, Sitting Bull had considered going to Canada. After all, he reasoned, many of the older men had hunted there, and before the American Revolution the Sioux had been British subjects. In fact, some of the chiefs had medals bearing the image of King George III, prizes given to them for fighting the Americans. So, as early as the previous summer, Sitting Bull had made up his mind. "We can find peace in the land of the Grandmother," he announced with hope.

Canada's reception of Sitting Bull and his people was at best lukewarm. The government's official position was that the "traversing of an imaginary boundary line by nomadic Indians in search of their means of subsistence is not an offense against international law." In other words, the authorities would not interfere with the Sioux, or attempt to expel them; the Sioux would be tolerated and allowed to stay as long as they obeyed the laws and caused no trouble. On the other hand, Canada did not offer Sitting Bull any help.

Sitting Bull and his band joined the refugee encampment of the elderly chief, Black Moon, in what is

Colonel Miles, known to the Indians as Bear Coat, agreed to meet with Sitting Bull on the plains, unarmed, midway between the Sioux warriors and the U.S. troops. Before the conference, Miles concealed a pistol under his great bear coat.

present-day southwestern Saskatchewan province. Altogether, the camp contained about 400 lodges. During the first year of their Canadian exile, Sitting Bull's followers were able to find sufficient food. Perhaps more importantly, they were free from the fears that haunted them in the United States.

Still, life in Canada fell short of that to which Sitting Bull was accustomed. The Indians' existence was based on land; only huge expanses, hundreds of square miles in size, could provide enough game to sustain the life of the band. However, the Canadian tribes were already making full use of the Canadian Plains. Competition for buffalo was intense. Once, these Sioux would have fought to increase their hunting range, as Sitting Bull had done in his days as chief of the Strong Hearts. But now, in the land of the Grandmother, this was no longer possible; if Sitting Bull's followers tried to make war on other tribes, the Canadian authorities would expel them.

To the government of the United States, Sitting Bull, living freely north of the border, was a dangerous symbol of Indian self-determination and resistance — or, in the government's view, subversion. In October 1878, a commission headed by General Alfred H. Terry and consisting of American political and military officials, as well as representatives of Canada's Royal North-West Mounted Police (RNWMP), was dispatched to Canada. Its mission was to offer Sitting Bull and his followers a general pardon if they would agree to surrender and return to the States.

Naturally, Sitting Bull was reluctant to meet with Terry's commission. "There is no use in talking to these Americans; they are all liars," he told RNWMP lieutenant colonel James F. MacLeod, "you cannot believe anything they say. . . . We have no faith in their promises." As if to justify his distrust, on the very day that an RNWMP

Sitting Bull's portrayal of his fight with Brave Indian, one of Colonel Miles's Indian scouts. Miles was pursuing Sitting Bull and his people, who were traveling to Canada in flight from the U.S. troops. Brave Indian was far ahead of the soldiers, following the Sioux too closely, when Sitting Bull turned back and killed him.

inspector was trying to persuade Sitting Bull to meet the commission, a band of about 100 Nez Percé Indians, wounded and bleeding, arrived at the camp. They had just escaped from U.S. troops led by Miles, who was now a general. Many of their relatives, including several respected leaders, had not been so lucky. They were killed by Miles's men. Sitting Bull was moved by the refugees' story; to him, it was both further evidence of American treachery and a warning of what awaited his people should they return.

Finally, however, Sitting Bull agreed to meet with the commission on October 17. As he entered the conference in Fort Walsh, the defiant chief warmly shook hands with his friend Colonel MacLeod and the other Canadians but walked past the American commissioners with disdain. General Terry spoke in a conciliatory manner, attempting to assure Sitting Bull that neither he nor his followers would in any way be harmed or punished if they surrendered. Terry insisted that "the Great Father [the president] . . . desires to live in peace with all his people. Too much white and Indian blood has already been shed. It is time that bloodshed should cease."

However, Terry's appeal was in vain. For too long

Sitting Bull's people had endured abuse and repression at the hands of the United States government and its troops. "What have we done that you should want us to stop?" the chief retorted. "We have done nothing. It is all the people on your side who started us to making trouble. We could go nowhere else, so we took refuge here."

Next, Sitting Bull introduced a series of speakers, all of whom endorsed his position. Finally, he rose to leave. "Shall I say to the president that you refuse the offers he has made you?" Terry asked him. "I have no more to say," Sitting Bull shot back. "This side of the boundary does not belong to your people. You belong on the other side; I belong here." The council adjourned, its mission a total failure.

After the meeting, Colonel MacLeod, at the commission's request, conferred with Sitting Bull. MacLeod explained his government's policy toward the Hunkpapas. He told Sitting Bull that his people were considered American Indians. As such, they were not British subjects and could expect nothing from the queen's government except protection as long as they abided by the laws. "Your only hope are the buffalo," MacLeod stated bluntly, "and it will not be many years before that source of supply will cease. You must not cross the border with hostile intent. If you do you will not only have the Americans for your enemies, but also the Mounted Police and the British government." MacLeod's gloomy words did not change Sitting Bull's mind; he would remain in the land of the Grandmother.

Sitting Bull's band endured four bitter Canadian winters. Each year, the buffalo herds dwindled. The Canadian parliament, as MacLeod had warned, would give them neither food nor clothing. Their only source of additional food and supplies was south of the border. Bands of warriors would cross into the United States, shoot some buffalo or raid the horse herds of the Crows, and then vanish into Canada. The U.S. Army, however, patrolled the region north of the Yellowstone, continually engaging the Indians in battle and driving them back across the border.

For much of the time, Sitting Bull's people lived on the edge of starvation. They also suffered for lack of shelter and blankets. Although at one point the band grew to more than 1,000, the almost constant hard times eroded Sitting Bull's ability to keep his followers together. More and more of his followers were leaving the camp and crossing the border into Dakota, where they surrendered at the Sioux agencies. Even Gall and Crow King, two of his most trusted lieutenants, gave up.

By the summer of 1881, the plight of Sitting Bull and the remnants of his original following had become hopeless. At Wood Mountain, Sitting Bull, in desperation, pleaded with RNWMP inspector A. R. Macdonnell for rations to feed his starving people. The inspector refused; he had his orders. Then, Sitting Bull threatened to collect his warriors and take the supplies by force. It was a feeble attempt at a bluff, however, and Macdonnell knew it. "Go ahead and try it," he dared the chief. Sitting Bull was beaten. He threw up his hands and cried, "I am thrown away!" There was only one thing left to do. He had to surrender for the sake of his people.

The next day, July 10, Sitting Bull and 186 of his followers began their sad journey across the border. All along the way the trails were littered with the bodies of buffalo, killed wantonly and wastefully by white hunters, not for food, but for sport — for fun. Shortly after his arrival in Canada four years earlier, Sitting Bull, in an interview published in the *New York Herald*, criticized the buffalo slaughter and the threat it posed to the Indians' very survival. "We kill buffaloes," he explained,

A woodcut by Berghaus of whites shooting buffalo on the Kansas-Pacific Railroad. Military personnel as well as civilians killed buffalo for sport, often with government-supplied ammunition. Secretary of the Interior Columbus Delano told Congress that he saw the "destruction of such game as Indians subsist upon as facilitating the policy of the Government . . . , compelling [the Indians] to begin to adopt the habits of civilization."

"as we kill other animals, for food and clothing, and to make our lodges warm. They kill buffaloes — for what? Go through [the] country. See the thousands of carcasses rotting on the Plains. Your young men shoot for pleasure. . . . You call us savages. What are *they*?" Four years later, surveying this blood-poisoned prairie, he realized that the life of the Sioux could never be what it once was.

The pathetic band arrived, tired, hungry, and dispirited, at Fort Buford at midday on July 19. One of the army officers who met them observed Sitting Bull's condition. Clad in a tattered calico shirt, shabby leggings, and a dirty blanket, the once-mighty chief looked old and beaten. "The final surrender of his cherished independence was a hard blow to his pride," the officer noted, "and he took it hard. He was much broken."

Sitting Bull surrendered his arms and his horses; in return, he was to receive a pardon for his past. He knew

Sitting Bull with his ninth wife (seated to his right) and three of their six children, at Fort Randall. It had always been a custom among members of the Sioux warrior societies to attempt to steal other men's wives, but no one was ever able to steal one of Sitting Bull's.

he had done nothing wrong, except that he had tried to live the life of his grandfathers, the life of a Sioux warrior. But his people were starving, and he was in no position to argue.

For these Indians, turning over their horses was perhaps the cruelest blow. At the end of the Civil War, even the victorious Union general, Ulysses S. Grant, allowed the men of his vanquished Confederate opponent, Robert E. Lee, to keep their horses. The beaten Sioux, however, were not allowed even that privilege. Stripped of their weapons and mounts, the Sioux also were stripped of their dignity. "My boy," Sitting Bull told his eight-year-old son, Crowfoot, "if you live, you will never be a man in this world, because you can never have a gun or a pony." Sitting Bull's deep pessimism cried out in these words to his boy: "if you live."

At Fort Buford, Sitting Bull and his followers boarded a steamboat, ironically named *The General Sherman,* for a trip down the Missouri. They had been led to believe that they were going to Fort Yates near the Hunkpapa agency at Standing Rock on the Grand River, not far from Sitting Bull's birthplace. There, they expected, they would be reunited with family and friends. But as was its habit, the United States government once again broke its promise to the Indians. Instead, Sitting Bull and his people were sent to Fort Randall. There they would be detained until the authorities were convinced that returning them to the Grand River area would not cause a disturbance. They were held at the fort for nearly two years.

Nevertheless, Sitting Bull's two years in confinement were not altogether unhappy ones. He was liked and admired by the officers at Fort Randall, who treated him with the respect that a chief deserved. Many of them expressed regret over the wrongs that the government and the army had committed against the Indians. People from around the world wrote him letters of praise and sympathy. Sioux leaders came to him for advice on political matters. Although a prisoner of war, Sitting Bull was regaining the self-assured, composed manner for which he previously had been known. A newspaper reporter who met him during this period remarked on the "inexpressible dignity in the strong face of the old chieftain," and his "general sense of reserved power, which expressed the born commander of men."

Finally, on May 10, 1883, the government decided that Sitting Bull and his followers no longer posed a threat to order. They were released and sent "home" to the Standing Rock Agency. Sitting Bull, once an independent and powerful Sioux war chief, had roamed the Great Plains without restraint; now 52 years old, he was compelled to settle down and live out a sedentary existence on the reservation.

7

THE LAST INDIAN

Life on the Standing Rock Reservation forced a series of drastic changes on the Plains Indians. The adults, who once hunted and gathered food for themselves, now went to the agency office to receive their rations. Their children came home from school with their hair cut short and their head filled with new ideas that challenged the wisdom of their elders, those centuries-old traditions that composed the heritage of the Sioux. Agency regulations forbade most ancient rites and practices. Dances were permitted only under close supervision. Christian missionaries sought to convert the people from their so-called heathen religious beliefs.

The once-mighty warrior societies were gone. In their place, an Indian police force, consisting of members of the tribe who were loyal to the white authorities, kept order on the government's behalf. Cooperative chiefs, like Gall and John Grass, who once were followers of Sitting Bull, now promoted the wishes of the Indian agent among their people. Sitting Bull was distressed; the life that he loved and fought for was dying.

In 1882, while Sitting Bull was still being held at Fort Randall, a government commission swept through the Sioux agencies. Through means that were scandalously dishonest, even by the government's standards, the commissioners managed to coax the Sioux leaders into ceding

some 14,000 square miles, about half the land in the Great Sioux Reservation, to the United States. But before Congress could act, a number of people in and out of government arose to question the commission's methods. A select committee of the Senate, headed by Senator Henry L. Dawes of Massachusetts, was dispatched to investigate the conditions of the Indian tribes in the northern Plains.

By the time the Dawes Commission reached the Standing Rock Agency, Sitting Bull had been released from his confinement and had joined his people on the reservation. By their behavior, it was unclear whether the commissioners were interested in righting past wrongs or in whitewashing them. The commissioners interrogated Indian witnesses into bewilderment and disregarded the grievances that the speakers voiced. All the while, Sitting Bull sat, waiting his turn to speak and seething with frustration.

Finally, the chairman, Senator Dawes, called upon Sitting Bull. Wasting no time, Dawes insulted Sitting

A photo taken at Fort Yates in 1875 of the first school erected on Standing Rock Indian Reservation. Government schools worked to assimilate Indians into American society.

Bull, refusing to recognize him as the chief of the Sioux. All right, thought the proud Sitting Bull, he would have to show them who was chief. So, in his most regal manner, he told the senators, "You have conducted yourselves like men who have been drinking whiskey, and I came here to give some advice." With that, he waved his hand, rose, and led all the Indians out of the room. Only the commissioners, their staff, and Standing Rock agent James McLaughlin were left.

It was an impressive and, to the white officials, frightening demonstration of Sitting Bull's power over his people and his potential to disrupt the government's Indian policy. Afterward, however, other Sioux leaders argued with the chief that he might have made a mistake. Perhaps one of these men would become the Grandfather, the president; to offend him only would cause more trouble for the Sioux. And, they added, these men were not out to steal Sioux lands but actually wanted to help the Indians get their land back. Sitting Bull was not convinced of the commission's trustworthiness. However, as an experienced diplomat, he agreed that he might have been lacking in tact and offered to apologize to the senators.

Another council was convened. Sitting Bull began his address to the meeting on a conciliatory note. "I came in," he explained, "with a glad heart to shake hands with you, my friends, for I feel that I have displeased you; and I am here to apologize to you for my bad conduct and to take back what I have said." He followed his apology with a long statement recounting the government's broken promises to the Indians, defending his actions on behalf of his people, and outlining a list of demands.

This time it was the commissioners' turn to be ungracious. Senator John Logan of Illinois attacked Sitting Bull on behalf of the group. "I want to say . . . that you are not a great chief of this country," Logan admonished him, "that you have no following, no power, no control, and no right to any control. . . . If it were not for the government you would be freezing and starving today in the mountains. . . . The government feeds and clothes and educates your children now, and desires to teach you to become farmers, and to civilize you, and *make you as white men*." But the senator's harangue meant nothing to Sitting Bull, and he managed to get in the last word. "If a man is a chief," he retorted, his dignity intact, "and has authority, he should be proud, and consider himself a great man."

At the Standing Rock Reservation, the official whose job it was to make the Sioux, in the words of Senator Logan, "as white men" was Indian agent James Mc-Laughlin. Most Indian agents had gotten their jobs through political connections, but possessed few other qualifications. McLaughlin, however, was experienced, intelligent, dedicated, and honest. He knew the Indians, and counted many as his friends; they called him "White Hair."

McLaughlin's idea of what was good for the Indians was unabashedly paternalistic. The Indians, he believed, should be "individualized," cut loose from the authority of the tribe, and taught to support themselves and their families by farming. Moreover, they should be Christianized as well as "Americanized," that is, trained to assume the rights and obligations of loyal citizens of the United States. McLaughlin worked hard to inculcate these white man's concepts of "culture" and "civilization" in the Sioux. Of course, to accomplish this, he would have to destroy the Sioux's own culture and civilization.

McLaughlin had been in charge of the Standing Rock Agency for about two years before Sitting Bull was moved there. During that time, his plan to transform these wandering hunters into sedentary farmers encountered little opposition from the Indian leaders. Chiefs like Gall and John Grass (Charging Bear), a Blackfoot Sioux, accepted the agent's forced acculturation scheme.

Once he arrived at Standing Rock, however, Sitting Bull stubbornly resisted McLaughlin's efforts to turn him and his followers into imitation white men. Naturally, there was friction between them from the start. McLaughlin correctly saw Sitting Bull as a threat to his program; Sitting Bull correctly saw McLaughlin as a threat to his people's way of life.

The determined agent never could win over, or beat down, the unyielding chief. Indeed, this failure blinded McLaughlin to Sitting Bull's true character and singular place in history. Throughout his memoir, *My Friend the Indian*, he described Sitting Bull as a coward and a fraud and claimed that he lacked support among the Sioux people. Even today, much that is written and said about Sitting Bull is clouded by McLaughlin's unsubstantiated, spiteful attacks.

In a photo taken by David F. Barry in 1886, Sitting Bull and Commissioner James McLaughlin stand opposite each other during the dedication of the Standing Rock at Standing Rock Agency. Although Sitting Bull was said to be cordial and charming to white visitors on the reservation, he resisted all of McLaughlin's efforts to Americanize the Sioux.

After the Dawes Commission fiasco, McLaughlin did everything in his power to diminish Sitting Bull's influence over the Standing Rock Sioux. He set up rival chiefs, like Gall and John Grass, men who curried favor with him and supported his ideas, and then he tried to ignore Sitting Bull. However, this had little impact on Sitting Bull's popularity with the Sioux; he remained their chosen leader. Moreover, it was Sitting Bull first and foremost that visitors to the agency, non-Indian as well as Indian, wanted to meet.

As long as he remained on the reservation, Sitting Bull was a constant symbol of resistance to McLaughlin's program to "civilize" the Sioux. So, McLaughlin encouraged Sitting Bull to travel as much as possible. The longer he was away, the agent reasoned, the less trouble he would cause.

In September 1883, Sitting Bull was chosen to make a welcoming speech at the dedication of the Northern Pacific Railroad in Bismarck, North Dakota. An army officer who knew the Sioux language was assigned to assist Sitting Bull in the preparation of his address. The chief would deliver the speech in his own language; afterward, the officer was to translate his words into English.

It was an ironic situation. All his life, Sitting Bull had regarded the railroad as a hated symbol of the destruction of his beloved Plains. The fouling of the environment, the slaughter of the buffalo, the uprooting of his people — all of these things had been done for mercenary reasons, to make profits for big business tycoons in the East. This was not something to be celebrated.

On the day of the ceremony Sitting Bull delivered his own speech, one that none of the white people, except the translator, could understand. He said, "I hate all white people. You are thieves and liars. You have taken away our land and made us outcasts." Occasionally, he would

John Grass, of the Blackfoot Sioux, curried favor with McLaughlin and was set up by the agent as a rival to the great head chief. However, Sitting Bull's power and influence remained intact, and every visitor to the reservation continued to ask to meet him.

pause, bow, smile, while the audience applauded, and then unleash more insults. Once he finished his private tirade and sat down, the bewildered officer, realizing that he could not translate Sitting Bull's diatribe, delivered the prepared version of the speech to a standing ovation. Sitting Bull had played quite a joke on the white politicians and railroad men; they enjoyed his address so much that they took him to another ceremony in St. Paul, Minnesota, for a repeat performance.

Sitting Bull's travels continued throughout the next two years. In 1883, he led the last Teton Sioux buffalo hunt. During 1884, he embarked on a 15-city tour with the showman, Colonel Alvaren Allen, on which he was falsely billed as "the slayer of General Custer." (The record of history is unclear as to who actually delivered the fatal blows to Custer; nevertheless, it could not have been Sitting Bull, who remained behind to defend the Hunkpapa camp from an expected second attack by Major Reno's battalion.)

In 1885, Sitting Bull toured the United States and Canada as a featured attraction of Buffalo Bill Cody's Wild West Show. He listened to the boos and catcalls of the crowds, and then sold them autographed pictures of himself. Most of the money he made, according to the sharpshooter Annie Oakley, another of Cody's big stars, "went into the pockets of small, ragged boys." He told her that he could not understand how the whites could be so unmindful and uncaring toward their own poor. "The white man knows how to make everything," he observed sadly, "but he does not know how to distribute it." Sitting Bull finished the season and came home with a present from his friend Buffalo Bill — a gray circus horse.

McLaughlin continued to do his best to keep Sitting Bull traveling — and out of his distinctive white hair. In 1886, he arranged for the chief to go to the Crow agency

A publicity poster for Colonel Alvaren Allen's 15-city tour, featuring Sitting Bull in combination with Spotted Horn Bull. Commissioner McLaughlin encouraged Sitting Bull to travel, thinking that his absence would abate his influence at Standing Rock Agency.

In 1885, Sitting Bull toured with Buffalo Bill Cody's Wild West Show throughout the United States and Canada. He declined going to England with Buffalo Bill because he felt that he was needed at home to help prevent the breakup of the Great Sioux Reservation.

in Montana. There Sitting Bull and his companions swapped memories and made peace with their old enemies. However, in 1887, when Buffalo Bill invited Sitting Bull to accompany him and the show to England, the chief declined. "I am needed here; there is more talk of taking our lands," he explained.

His refusal annoyed McLaughlin. Not only would the agent have Sitting Bull on his hands, but he now realized that the chief's previous travels actually served to increase his prestige and authority among the Standing Rock Sioux.

His position secure, Sitting Bull resisted McLaughlin at every turn — refusing to give up polygamy, fighting the attempt to ban medicine men, resisting the drive to convert the Sioux to the Christian religion. As an alternative to the agent's plan, he formulated his own program for the Sioux: self-support, education, a reunited nation, and a return to traditional religious beliefs and practices. He settled in a log cabin close to his birthplace near the Grand River, where he farmed, raised cattle and chickens, and did all he could to frustrate McLaughlin.

In 1888, a government commission arrived at Standing Rock to arrange the breakup of the Great Sioux Reservation into six smaller ones. It also offered to buy 11 million acres of Sioux land for the shamefully low price of 50 cents an acre. Sitting Bull managed to line up all four of McLaughlin's pet chiefs — Gall, John Grass, and the Yanktonais Mad Bear and Big Head — against this attempted swindle. The commissioners could get no more than 22 of the adult men at Standing Rock to sign the agreement, far short of the three-fourths required by the Treaty of Laramie. They were equally unsuccessful at the

Members of Sitting Bull's family stand outside his cabin, situated near the Grand River.

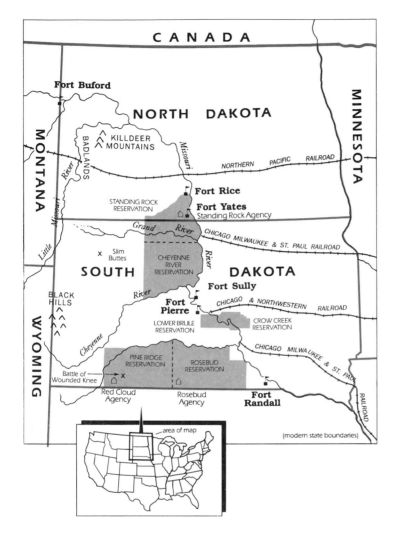

CANADA

MINNESOTA

Fort Buford

NORTH DAKOTA

MONTANA

KILLDEER
MOUNTAINS

BADLANDS

Missouri River

NORTHERN   PACIFIC   RAILROAD

Fort Rice
Fort Yates
Standing Rock Agency

STANDING ROCK
RESERVATION

Grand   River

CHICAGO   MILWAUKEE & ST. PAUL RAILROAD

x Slim
Buttes

CHEYENNE
RIVER
RESERVATION

SOUTH   DAKOTA

Fort Sully

BLACK
HILLS

River

Fort
Pierre

CHICAGO & NORTHWESTERN   RAILROAD

WYOMING

Cheyenne

LOWER BRULE
RESERVATION

CROW CREEK
RESERVATION

CHICAGO MILWAUKEE & ST. PAUL

PINE RIDGE
RESERVATION

ROSEBUD
RESERVATION

RAILROAD

Battle of
Wounded Knee

Red Cloud
Agency

Rosebud
Agency

Fort
Randall

area of map

(modern state boundaries)

In 1889, despite Sitting Bull's efforts to stop the Sioux from signing away their land, government officials left Standing Rock with more signatures than required by the Treaty of 1868, allowing a cession that broke up the Great Sioux Reservation.

other agencies. When they returned to Washington, they recommended that the government simply ignore the 1868 treaty and take the land without the Indians' consent.

The government, however, was not ready to take such a drastic step — not yet. Sitting Bull and a delegation were brought to Washington. There the chief stood up to the secretary of the interior and extracted an agreement from him that *if* the Teton Sioux ceded any of their land, they would receive no less than $1.25 an acre. He shook hands with the president, and returned home, his influence reaffirmed. Back at the reservation, Sitting Bull spoke out against the sale of Sioux lands at any price.

The following summer, Sitting Bull's old adversary, General "Three Stars" Crook, brought another commission to the Sioux reservations, attempting to buy the lands at the new price. He encountered token resistance from Red Cloud's Oglala followers at the Pine Ridge Reservation, but even there, about half of the adult men signed the cession agreement. At Rosebud and the smaller reservations, the chiefs led their people to sign away the lands. Standing Rock was Crook's last stop; there the deal would succeed or fail.

Sitting Bull, his influence on the reservation at its height, was able to block Three Stars, throwing the entire land sale in jeopardy. Frustrated, Crook told McLaughlin to do whatever was necessary to complete the deal. Through a series of secret meetings, the agent managed to coerce his puppet chiefs to abandon Sitting Bull. Gall, John Grass, and the others stood behind the agent when he threatened to withhold all rations until the agreement was ratified. In his ultimate act of deceit, McLaughlin concealed the next commission meeting from Sitting Bull and his followers. When they arrived late, the Indian police tried to prevent them from attending the most important council in the history of the Sioux nation.

Sitting Bull forced his way through the police line and into the council circle. He charged that no one told him about the meeting. Crook asked McLaughlin, "Did Sitting Bull know we were going to hold a council?" "Yes, Sir," the agent lied, "Everybody knew it." At that moment, the chiefs led their people in signing the agreement. The Great Sioux Reservation had been broken up. As he left the grounds, a newspaper reporter asked Sitting Bull what he thought of all this. "Indians!" the chief answered in disgust. "There are no Indians left but me!"

*Indian police at Standing
Rock, photographed by David
F. Barry.*

8

A MARKED MAN

Sitting Bull had warned the people that, as before, the white politicians would not keep their promises. The Indians had sold their land, but they still had not received the money to which they were entitled. Not only were their rations not increased, as Crook had pledged, they were actually reduced by 20 percent. Then, in 1890, a drought made farming impossible. At every agency hunger was followed by starvation, with disease and death close behind.

By the autumn of 1890, a new religion, called the "Ghost Dance," was sweeping the reservations. Started in the West by a Paiute Indian prophet named Wovoka, its doctrines combined traditional Indian religion with aspects of the Christian faith. Its central teaching was that the Messiah, Jesus Christ, was returning to earth. Because the whites had denied and killed him, this time the Savior would appear in the body of an Indian. Bringing buffalo and horses, he would unite all Indians of all nations, living and dead. The new earth would be for the Indians only; the whites would be removed by supernatural means. In order to bring about this millennium, the faithful were required to dance the Ghost Dance regularly until the arrival of their Messiah.

Kicking Bear, a Minneconjou Sioux from the Cheyenne River Reservation, brought the news to Sitting Bull's

camp. The chief listened with interest. Historians debate as to how much of the doctrine Sitting Bull actually accepted. He is said to have commented, with skepticism, "It is impossible for a dead man to return and live again." Still, his mystic inclinations must have been aroused by the new religion.

More importantly, Sitting Bull's starving, grieving Sioux had lost everything; the Ghost Dance promised to return to them everything they had lost: their horses, their buffalo, their land, their loved ones — their old life. It gave them hope in the midst of their deep despair. So, Sitting Bull allowed Kicking Bear to teach this new religion to his people.

Agent McLaughlin denounced the Ghost Dance and had Kicking Bear arrested and expelled from the reservation. In the agent's words, "A more pernicious system of religion could not have been offered to a people who stood on the threshold of civilization." Even though he was a practicing Catholic, McLaughlin could not see that

Sioux women wait for rations at Pine Ridge Agency in 1891. Sitting Bull had warned his people that the whites would break their promises. Indeed, after the cession of 1889, rations were reduced by 20 percent.

despite the Indian rituals, the new religion was essentially Christian in its content, particularly in its teaching of the Second Coming of the Messiah. Moreover, it taught the Christian doctrines of nonviolence and brotherly love to the Indians in ways that the missionaries never could.

But despite its spiritual nature, the Ghost Dance had arisen out of the Indians' real experiences of suffering and deprivation; it was the expression, in spiritual form, of their everyday life and their desire to change it. In short, the Ghost Dance had a political as well as a religious significance. Realizing this, Sitting Bull encouraged the Ghost Dance faithful to unite in opposition to the dreadful, worsening conditions on the reservation.

Years earlier, as a warrior, Sitting Bull had advocated military resistance against the whites. On the reservation, he had tried diplomatic means, until those proved fruitless. This new religion represented, for Sitting Bull, another form of resistance against the white authorities — spiritual resistance. Anxious that the Ghost Dance might kindle dissent among the Sioux, McLaughlin resolved to subdue both the religion and the man who, in his mind, was its main proponent — Sitting Bull.

Outside the reservation, rumors spread among the white settlers that the Sioux, revved into a frenzy by the Ghost Dance and riled into action by Sitting Bull, were about to launch a massacre against them. Their panic was unfounded. The Indians were both greatly outnumbered and poorly armed. It was because they lacked any real power of their own that they were calling on the Messiah to destroy the white men for them. In short, the Indians had much more to fear from the whites than vice versa. Nevertheless, both agency personnel and the military officers at nearby Fort Yates believed that Sitting Bull had enough support to precipitate a general uprising among the Sioux.

A participant in the Ghost Dance, photographed by James Mooney in 1893. The Ghost Dance arose from the Indians' suffering and expressed their desire for a better life. Realizing its political significance, Sitting Bull encouraged followers of the Ghost Dance religion to resist demands of whites.

At this point, Sitting Bull and his people became the pawns in a petty bureaucratic game between the Indian Bureau and the War Department. The acting commissioner of Indian affairs advised the secretary of the interior that Sitting Bull, the leading symbol of resistance to federal authority among the Sioux, should be arrested and confined to a military prison. McLaughlin was instructed to make plans for the seizure of Sitting Bull, and he readily complied. The Ghost Dance would now serve as a convenient excuse for the removal of Sitting Bull, who had been a thorn in the agent's side ever since the day he arrived at the reservation more than seven years earlier.

At the same time, President Benjamin Harrison directed the secretary of war to assume military responsibility for subduing the Ghost Dancers. General Miles, old Bear Coat, was put in command of the campaign. As in 1876, the year of the Little Bighorn debacle, a huge number of soldiers were transferred into Sioux country. Dr. Valentine McGillycuddy, the former Pine Ridge agent, criticized the military response as excessive. "If the Seventh-

Day Adventists prepare their ascension robes for the second coming of the Saviour," he observed, "the United States Army is not put into motion to prevent them. . . . If the troops remain, trouble is sure to come." The stage was set for another catastrophe; the U.S. government rarely deployed troops without using them in battle.

At Standing Rock, McLaughlin maintained that his Indian police could subdue the Ghost Dancers far more neatly and efficiently than the troops could. For political reasons, he needed to reassert his authority over the agency. The newspapers already were reporting that McLaughlin had "lost control of his Indians." The presence of the army, he feared, would only reinforce that claim. And so for the next month, McLaughlin and the War Department bickered over how best to control the Sioux.

Miles, like McLaughlin, believed that Sitting Bull was the power behind the Ghost Dance at Standing Rock. Well aware of Sitting Bull's popularity, the general realized that a forced arrest by the army could cause trouble on the reservation. It must be done quietly, he insisted. And so, Miles called on the chief's old friend, Buffalo Bill Cody, one of the few white men that Sitting Bull trusted. "The whole secret of treating with [sic] Indians," the famous showman once explained, "is to be honest with them and do as you agree," a lesson that the government never learned.

Cody was sent to Standing Rock with orders to convince Sitting Bull to leave the reservation for a conference with Miles. It is unclear whether or not Buffalo Bill, on Miles's orders, was supposed to "arrest" Sitting Bull, as some historians have claimed. Likewise, it is unknown whether or not Cody knew that if he succeeded in his mission, Sitting Bull would have been confined to a military prison. Perhaps the showman wanted the publicity of being the man who arrested Sitting Bull; or perhaps he thought that by interceding he could save his friend from possible danger. In the end, however, his motives were irrelevant. McLaughlin, resenting this "interference" by the military, blocked Cody from ever seeing Sitting Bull.

As mid-December neared, McLaughlin began to report that, in his view, Sitting Bull was preparing to leave the reservation. Some 2,000 to 3,000 Sioux from the Pine Ridge, Rosebud, and Cheyenne River reservations had fled into the Dakota Badlands when the troops arrived. The agent feared that Sitting Bull would attempt to organize these fugitives, leading them in hostile actions against the white settlers and soldiers.

On December 11, Sitting Bull wrote to McLaughlin informing him that he intended to travel to Pine Ridge in order to investigate the Ghost Dance further. Sitting Bull's letter implied that he still had some doubts about the new religion. More important, his action to send this letter should have thrown McLaughlin's fears into question. If Sitting Bull really was leaving to organize a hostile band of refugee Indians, it is unlikely that he would inform an agent of the Indian Bureau of his departure.

McLaughlin received Sitting Bull's letter the next day. That same afternoon, another letter came, one that authorized Sitting Bull's arrest. Seeing his nemesis, Sitting Bull, about to slip through his fingers, McLaughlin decided to waste no time in making the arrest. On December 14, he instructed the Indian police to "make the arrest before daylight tomorrow." The agent ended his order with an ominous postscript: "You must not let him escape under any circumstances." One hundred men of the Eighth Cavalry from Fort Yates were deployed to support the police, if necessary. McLaughlin, however much he spoke of avoiding bloodshed, was clearly preparing for it.

Before dawn on the morning of December 15, 1890, 39 Indian policemen and 4 volunteers rode into the camp of Sitting Bull. They entered the chief's cabin, awoke him and placed him under arrest. While he dressed before being taken away, a crowd began to form outside the cabin. The police tried to escort Sitting Bull, quite roughly, out the door and onto his horse, but the mob, growing by the minute, blocked them. The situation was tense and dangerous, with the police outnumbered four to one.

Sitting Bull resisted. "Do with me what you like," he cried. "I am not going." Then to his people he called, "Come on! Come on! Take action! Let's go!" His followers were waiting for this order. The head of Sitting Bull's bodyguard, Catch-the-Bear, raised his rifle and shot the Indian police commander, Lieutenant Bullhead, in the leg. As Bullhead went down, he shot Sitting Bull in

The letter from James Mc-Laughlin instructing the Indian police to arrest Sitting Bull. The postscript reads, "You must not let him escape under any circumstances."

the left side. At about the same time, Sergeant Red Tomahawk also fired and struck the chief in the head. Sitting Bull fell, killed instantly.

A bloody melee ensued. Only the arrival of the troops saved the Indian police from complete annihilation by the enraged mob. The Indians had no desire to engage in battle with the better-armed soldiers. Perhaps if the army had been sent in to apprehend Sitting Bull, his followers would not have resisted or fought back, and their chief's life would have been spared. McLaughlin, however, insisted on using his Indian police "to avert bloodshed."

When the smoke finally cleared, Sitting Bull's lifeless body was surrounded by those of his loyal bodyguard, including his adopted brother, Jumping Bull, and his 17-year-old son, Crowfoot. In all, seven of his band had died alongside their chief. Six of the Indian police, including Bullhead, also lost their life.

President Benjamin Harrison expressed relief when he learned of Sitting Bull's death; according to the *New York Herald*, the president "had regarded Sitting Bull as the great disturbing element in his tribe, and now that he was out of the way he hoped that a settlement of the difficulties could be reached without further bloodshed." A far more fitting epitaph was offered by Major James Morrow Walsh, a retired officer of the RNWMP who became a friend of Sitting Bull's during the chief's Canadian exile. Walsh said that Sitting Bull's death represented "a nation against one man. . . . The one man was murdered by the nation to destroy the principle he advocated — that no man against his will should be forced to be a beggar. Sitting Bull was the marked man of his people."

Two weeks after Sitting Bull made his last stand, his people made theirs. On the morning of December 29,

Crowfoot, Sitting Bull's son, photographed by David F. Barry. Shot during the struggle with the Indian police at Sitting Bull's cabin, Crowfoot died alongside his father.

1890, a camp of about 350 Sioux refugees were being held by the cavalry near Wounded Knee Creek. The soldiers were supposed to escort these Sioux back to the Pine Ridge Reservation, but suddenly, in a moment of panic and confusion, the soldiers fired upon the Indians. More than 150 Sioux were killed immediately, and almost as many more died later, either from their wounds or from exposure to the cold. Most of the dead were women, children, and unarmed men. (Twenty-five soldiers also died, most of them struck by their own bullets or shrapnel.) The government had won; never again would Indians offer any resistance against the encroachment of the white man's notion of "civilization."

And so, the story of Sitting Bull paralleled the history of the Plains Indians. Their triumphs and heroics were his, as were their sufferings and ultimate demise. Sitting Bull lived a tradition of self-determination and independence, in defense of an ancient and cherished heritage. His death, like the massacre at Wounded Knee just 14 days later, was not so different from the fate suffered by other proud Indians who, like him, refused to abandon their principles and accept a foreign way of life.

CHRONOLOGY

1831	Born near present-day town of Bullhead, South Dakota
1845	Joins war party and counts first coup; receives the name Sitting Bull from his father
1856	Kills Crow chief in combat; becomes chief of the Strong Hearts warrior society
1857	Adopts captive Assiniboin boy as a brother
1864	Participates in the Battle of Killdeer Mountain and the Battle of the Badlands
1865	Fights U.S. troops in the Battle of Powder River
1867	Inaugurated head chief of the Teton Sioux
1868	Negotiates the Treaty of Laramie with Father Pierre Jeane De Smet
1869	Spares Frank Grouard and adopts him as a brother
1876	Assembles a force of Plains Indians and prepares for war against the U.S. Army; performs the Sun Dance ritual and prophesies victory; defeats General Crook in the Battle of the Rosebud; defeats General Custer in the Battle of Little Bighorn; meets with Colonel Miles
1877	Takes his people to Canada
1878	Meets with U.S. commission and refuses to leave Canada
1881	Returns with his people to the United States and surrenders at Fort Buford
1881–83	Held in confinement at Fort Randall
1883	Released from Fort Randall and transferred to Standing Rock Agency; denounces the Dawes Commission
1885	Travels throughout the United States and Canada with Buffalo Bill Cody's Wild West Show
1888	Resists the proposed breakup of the Great Sioux Reservation
1889	Attempts unsuccessfully to block cession of land to the government
1890	Killed by the Standing Rock Indian police during an attempted arrest, two weeks before the massacre at Wounded Knee Creek

FURTHER READING

Adams, Alexander B. *Sitting Bull: An Epic of the Plains.* New York: Putnam, 1973.

Brown, Dee. *Bury My Heart at Wounded Knee.* New York: Washington Square Press, 1981.

Debo, Angie. *A History of the Indians of the United States.* Norman: University of Oklahoma Press, 1989.

Hoover, Herbert T. "Sitting Bull." In *American Indian Leaders: Studies in Diversity*, edited by R. David Edmunds. Lincoln: University of Nebraska Press, 1980.

Sandoz, Mari. *The Battle of Little Bighorn.* Lincoln: University of Nebraska Press, 1978.

Taylor, Colin. *The Warriors of the Plains.* New York: Arco, 1975.

Tillett, Leslie, ed. *Wind on the Buffalo Grass: The Indians' Own Accounts of the Battle at Little Bighorn River and the Death of Their Life on the Plains.* New York: Crowell, 1976.

Utley, Robert M. *The Last Days of the Sioux Nation.* New Haven: Yale University Press, 1963.

Utley, Robert M., and Wilcomb E. Washburn. *Indian Wars.* Boston: Houghton Mifflin, 1987.

Vestal, Stanley. *Sitting Bull: Champion of the Sioux.* Norman: University of Oklahoma Press, 1989.

Wooster, Robert. *The Military and United States Indian Policy, 1865–1903.* New Haven: Yale University Press, 1988.

INDEX

PICTURE CREDITS

The Bettmann Archive, pages 2, 45, 47, 81, 84; Courtesy of the Buffalo Bill Historical Center, Cody, WY, pages 38, 92; Custer Battlefield National Monument, page 65; Denver Public Library, Western History Department, pages 75 (photo by Geo. E. Spencer, Fort Sheridan), 96 (photo by David F. Barry), 98; Library of Congress, pages 54, 68; Minnesota Historical Society, page 15; National Anthropological Archives, Smithsonian Institution, pages 13 (photo # 3199-C-11), 20 (photo # 3195-G), 24 (photo # 3199-D-1), 52 (photo # 3199-E-7), 60 (photo # 3199-D-17), 78 (photo # F3199-C-15), 89 (photo # 56650); The National Archives, pages 56, 76; The National Cowboy Hall of Fame and Western Heritage Center, Oklahoma City, pages 40–41; Courtesy of the Nebraska State Historical Society, page 50; Photograph courtesy of the Smithsonian Institution, National Museum of the American Indian, pages 22 (neg. # 30773), 28 (neg. # 30769), 62 (neg. # 28921); The South Dakota Department of Tourism, pages 18–19; South Dakota State Historical Society, Pierre, SD, pages 10, 42, 63, 70, 72, 82, 100, 104; State Historical Society of North Dakota, pages 16, 21, 26, 30–31, 34, 86, 90, 91, 93, 103, 106; The University of Michigan Museum of Art, Bequest of Henry C. Lewis, 1895.80, page 44.

Maps (pages 48, 94) by Gary Tong.

PROPERTY OF
BOURBONNAIS PUBLIC LIBRARY

BOB BERNOTAS is a freelance writer living in New York City. He holds a doctorate in political theory from the Johns Hopkins University and has taught philosophy and political science at Morgan State and Towson State Universities. His published works include several books on American government, numerous articles on jazz and sports, and a biography of Amiri Baraka.

W. DAVID BAIRD is the Howard A. White Professor of History at Pepperdine University in Malibu, California. He holds a Ph.D. from the University of Oklahoma and was formerly on the faculty of history at the University of Arkansas, Fayetteville, and Oklahoma State University. He has served as president of both the Western History Association, a professional organization, and Phi Alpha Theta, the international honor society for students of history. Dr. Baird is also the author of *The Quapaw Indians: A History of the Downstream People* and *Peter Pitchlynn: Chief of the Choctaws* and the editor of *A Creek Warrior of the Confederacy: The Autobiography of Chief G. W. Grayson.*